The Oryx Multicultural Folktale Series

Tom Thumb

by
Margaret Read MacDonald

Illustrated by
Joanne Caroselli

ORYX PRESS
1993

Published by The Oryx Press
4041 North Central at Indian School Road
Phoenix, Arizona 85012-3397

Published simultaneously in Canada

Printed and bound in the United States of America

∞ The paper used in this publication meets the minimum requirements of American National Standard for Information Science—Permanence of Paper for Printed Library Materials, ANZI Z39.48, 1984.

A list of copyright statements for contributed material appears on page viii

Library of Congress Cataloging-in-Publication Data

Tom Thumb/ [collected] by Margaret Read MacDonald ; illustrated by
   Joanne Caroselli.
      p.   cm.—(The Oryx multicultural folktale series)
   Includes bibliographical references and index.
   Summary: Presents twenty-five variants of the "Tom Thumb" tale
from around the world, with notes on each, a unit for classroom
study, a bibliography, and suggestions for other related activities.
   ISBN 0-89774-728-3
   1. Tom Thumb (Tale)—Juvenile literature. [1. Fairy tales.
2. Folklore. 3. Tom Thumb (Tale)] I. MacDonald, Margaret Read,
1940– . II. Caroselli, Joanne, ill. III. Tom Thumb. English.
IV. Series.
GR75.T64T66 1993   93-21
398.21—dc20   CIP
                                                    AC

Contents

---

* Retold for ease in storytelling

Preface

A Thumbling Collection

Here are 25 stories featuring thumblings. Since the notion of a diminutive hero or heroine is popular throughout the world, sample thumbling tales from 21 cultures are collected here for your use.

An extensive selection of whole language activities are suggested to help you integrate the study of thumbling tales into many areas of your curriculum. To help you in cross cultural study of thumbling tales, comparative notes on the tales selected are provided, along with a bibliography of thumbling materials.

The author has retold four of these tales for ease in storytelling: "Loud Mouth Thummas," "Issun Boshi," "Little Thumb Conquers the Sun," and "Tough Little Niraidak." Other tales suggested for easy learning and telling are: "Lipuniushka" and "Hasan, the Heroic Mouse-Child." Any of these tales can be used with preschool and primary children as well as with upper elementary students. "Fereyel and Debbo Engal," "Digit the Midget," "Boy-Man," and "Piñoncito" are more lengthy and not so easy to learn, but would be fun to tell to primary and upper elementary students. Or you can simply read them aloud.

Junior high and high school students will find the bizarre love affairs of "Tough Little Niraidak" and "The Snail *Choja*" amusing and will be suitably disgusted by the Armenian "Mundig." This latter tale is included for its interest in cross cultural studies, but it would be considered unsuitable for most classroom use in the United States. A thumbling unit for these older students, of course, would be approached as a study in folklore comparisons.

How to Use This Collection

Skim through these 25 tales and pick out a few favorites. Read or tell them to your students. Share a picture book with the Grimm's version of Tom Thumb (see page 3). Begin a list of Tom Thumb's antics. Compare the tale you read, and talk about the way thumblings are used in stories.

Read over the suggested activities in the Whole Language Curriculum section and select a few that you think might be fun to share.

Note that the first 10 tales in this collection are variants of one tale, Type 700 *Tom Thumb*. Next come "Petit Poucet" and "Fereyel and Debbo Engal the Witch," which are variants of a different tale, Type 327 *The Children and the Ogre*. The remaining 12 tales show thumblings playing roles in several other stories.

Thumblings in Literature and Folklore

Miniature people have proved a fascinating topic in stories and novels written for children. Tiny families such as Mary Norton's *The Borrowers* and John Peterson's *The Littles* are perennially popular. Small heroes such as Eric Kästner's *Little Man* show one small individual in a larger environment. And often mice are introduced as main characters, in a successful attempt to pit tiny creatures against a larger universe. Margery Sharp's *The Rescuers*, Robert O'Brien's *Mrs. Frisby and the Rats of NIMH*, and Jean Van Leeuwen's *The Great Rescue Operation* are a few examples. Perhaps most compelling of all are those tales of lone mice attempting to survive in a human-size world. William Steig's *Abel's Island*, T. H. White's *Stuart Little*, and the boy-turned-mouse in Roald Dahl's *The Witches* all capture our hearts as well as our curiosity.

Folk tellers too have wondered what it would be like for a very tiny person to survive in a huge world. The Tom Thumb story had appeared in print by 1621 in England. The version printed then was an elaborate retelling with many poetic interludes. The story had probably been around a long time as a hearthside tale before it found its way into print. In this basic Tom Thumb tale Tom's parents wish for a son, even if he is only as big as a thumb. They get their wish. Tom's wee size enables him to have many strange adventures. He gets lost in his mother's pudding, is eaten by a cow, manages to steer a horse by hiding in its ear, is carried away by a bird...the possibilities are endless, and various editions of this tale just add more and more adventures.

The idea of a small Tom Thumb was so intriguing that other stories began to introduce a character called Tom Thumb as their hero too. Usually these "Tom Thumbs" were not thumb size but were very small persons. In a tale written down by Charles Perrault, Tom Thumb is the youngest and tiniest of seven brothers. This "Petit Poucet" (Little Thumb) overcomes his brothers' rejection by rescuing them from an ogre. In England this tale was reprinted as "Hop O' My Thumb."

In Germany Tom Thumb has been told in several variations. In addition to the usual thumbling tales, the Grimms collected "Thumbling the Dwarf" and "Thumbling the Giant." In this tale the small thumbling is raised by a giant and becomes a giant himself!

Because of Tom Thumb's small size, he functions well as a trickster. Larger adversaries are defeated by his wits. This trickster quality gives him some kinship with other tricksters of world folklore. Theoretically Tom Thumb could be introduced as hero into any story of a small trickster. In this collection, for instance, you will see him as hero in a Burmese story of a wee fellow who swallows a clump of moss, a rotten egg, a bamboo thorn, and a boat and then spits them up to fight the sun.

Probably most intriguing of the Tom Thumb stories are those in which Tom is actually a miniature human. The problems of this three-inch-high man are a source of endless wonder. The teller's imagination wanders among household objects, placing Tom beside them and imagining how he would use them. The Japanese teller lets Issun Boshi use a rice bowl as a boat, a chopstick as an oar, a needle as a sword. The Russian teller shows Tom crawling out of a fluff of spinning cotton, and the British teller lets Tom fall into his mother's cooking.

And Tom, being so very tiny, keeps having outrageous adventures. Most horrendous he is often eaten by animals or humans! In cleaned-up contemporary versions he is usually quickly disgorged. But in earlier centuries poor Tom most often had to pass through the animal's digestive tract and drop out at the other end before his trials were over.

In only a few instances does our tale contain a female thumbling. Perhaps we should call her "Thumbelina" from Hans Christian Andersen's lovely tale. Andersen himself created many of his stories from folk themes, but embroidered them with his own wonderful fancy, turning them into literary gems. Thumbelina's adventures are similar in many ways to those of the male Tom Thumb, but this story seems a female, and much more genteel adventure.

And there are other female thumblings. "Doll in the Grass," a tale collected in Norway in the nineteenth century by Peter Asbjörnsen and Jörgen Moe, features a wee maid who assists a prince in search of the perfect bride. "Doll in the Grass" becomes a full-grown woman at the story's end and marries the prince. This story is popular throughout Europe but usually features a frog maid or other small animal. An unusual variant featuring a miniature girl has been collected in Vietnam as "Little Finger of the Watermelon Patch" (see *The Brocaded Slipper and Other Vietnamese Tales* by Lynette Dyer Vuong. New York: Harper Collins, 1982).

Thumblings in the Classroom

These thumbling tales offer many uses for a whole language web. The tales can be read aloud or distributed within the classroom for reading. Several of them will be enjoyed if told aloud. You may want to compare variants of Tom Thumb or Petit Poucet; several variants of each are included in this collection, and listings of other variants are given in the "Tale Notes" and in the bibliographies contained within this book. Speculation about the problems and successes of a small hero lead to creative writing. Creative dramatic enactments of a thumbling's adventures are also fun. The sharing of these Tom Thumb stories should lead children to read the many delightful novels featuring miniature heroes, and you should screen some of the delightful films about small characters as well. Discuss their artistic treatment of the material and their cinematic techniques.

Your science studies might explore the real world of miniature creatures. Or you might want to learn about dwarfism in humans and in plants and animals. Read about famous humans of small stature. Discuss social problems facing little people. Study small human groups such as the Mbuti and the San (Bushmen).

Expand the social studies element of your thumbling unit by examining the various cultures from which these tales come. Post a map and find the places from which these tales were collected. Look for elements within the tales that are specific to that culture. Include math in your thumbling studies with work in measurement and ratios. And plan physical games to experience smallness. Include art activities that help you think about size. Suggestions for these activities appear in the "Whole Language Curriculum for Tom Thumb" section at the end of this book, along with programs for use in the public library, and a multicultural index.

Learn More about Thumbling Tales

To prepare yourself for discussion of thumbling tales read the brief essay "Early Print Versions of Tom Thumb," (page 149) which will inform you about some early English uses of the tale, and scan the "Notes to the Tales" section (page 135). There the sources of these tales are noted and other variants are discussed. Also the extensive "Bibliography of Works Consulted" (page 170) goes beyond the mere listing of books cited here to include other thumbling tales for further study.

Have fun with your thumbling explorations. Use your imagination and THINK SMALL.

Acknowledgments to Contributors

Permission to reprint copyrighted material has been kindly granted by the following publications, organizations, and individuals.

Arnott, Kathleen. *African Myths & Legends.* Henry Z. Walck, 1962. ©1962 Kathleen Arnott.

"Fereyel and Debbo Engal" reprinted by permission of Random House, Inc.

Ashabranner, Brent and Russell Davis. *The Lion's Whiskers.* Little, Brown and Co., 1959. © 1959 Russell G. Davis and Brent K. Ashabranner.

"Digit the Midget" reprinted by permission of the authors.

Carey, Bonnie. *Baba Yaga's Geese.* Indiana University Press, 1973. © 1973 Indiana University Press.

"Lipuniushka" reprinted by permission of Indiana University Press.

Hoogosian-Villa, Susie. *100 Armenian Tales and Their Folkloristic Relevance.* Wayne State University, 1966. © 1966 Wayne State University Press.

"Mundig" reprinted by permission of Wayne State University Press.

Htin Aung, Maung. *Burmese Folk Tales.* Oxford University Press, 1948. © 1948 Oxford University Press.

"The Diminutive Flute Player" reprinted by permission of publisher.

Lang, Andrew. *The Yellow Fairy Book.* Dover, 1966.

"The Hazel-nut Child" reprinted by permission of publisher.

"Thumbelina" reprinted by permission of publisher.

Massignon, Geneviéve. *Folktales of France.* University of Chicago, 1960. © 1960 The University of Chicago Press.

"Tom Thumb" reprinted by permission of publisher.

Perrault, Charles. *Perrault's Fairy Tales.* Translated by A. E. Johnson. Dover, 1969.

"Little Tom Thumb" reprinted by permission of publisher. Retitled "Petit Poucet" in this edition.

Seki, Keigo. *Folktales of Japan.* University of Chicago, 1963. © 1963 The University of Chicago Press.

"The Snail *Choja*" reprinted by permission of publisher.

Wade, Mary Hazelton. *Indian Fairy Tales.* Core Collection, 1979.

"Boy-Man" reprinted by permission of Roth Publishing, Inc.

Walker, Barbara K. *A Treasury of Turkish Folktales for Children.* Linnet, 1988. © 1988 Barbara K. Walker.

"Hasan, the Heroic Mouse-Child" reprinted by permission of Shoe String Press, Inc.

Tales

Thumbling

A German tale from the Brothers Grimm

The Grimms' version of "Thumbling" seems a good tale with which to begin this compilation of thumbling tales. This is the basic folktale that we will see condensed, expanded, and altered in variants from other countries. This is not, however, the earliest version in this collection. The Grimms collected their tale in the early nineteenth century while the English Tom Thumb had been in print since 1621. This does not mean, however, that one tale was being told earlier than the other.

Several elements are common in many variants of this tale: Parents wish for a child even if no bigger than a thumb; Thumbling drives his father's horse; Thumbling is eaten by a cow; Thumbling falls in with robbers and tricks them. We will encounter these elements several times in the stories that follow.

*T*here was once a poor peasant who sat in the evening by the hearth and poked the fire, and his wife sat and span. Then said he, "How sad it is that we have no children! With us all is so quiet, and in other houses it is noisy and lively."

"Yes," replied the wife, and sighed, "even if we had only one, and it were quite small, and only as big as a thumb, I should be quite satisfied, and we would still love it with all our hearts." Now it so happened that the woman fell ill, and after seven months, gave birth to a child, that was perfect in all its limbs, but no longer than a thumb. Then said they, "It is as we wished it to be, and it shall be our dear child;" and because of its size, they called it Thumbling. They did not let it want for food, but the child did not grow taller, but remained as it had been at the first; nevertheless it looked sensibly out of its eyes, and soon showed itself to be a wise and nimble creature, for everything it did turned out well.

One day the peasant was getting ready to go into the forest to cut wood, when he said as if to himself, "How I wish that there was any one who would bring the cart to me!" "Oh, father," cried Thumbling, "I will soon bring the cart, rely on that; it shall be in the forest at the appointed time." The man smiled and said, "How can that be done, thou art far too small to lead the horse by the reins?" "That's of no consequence, father, if my mother will only harness it, I will sit in the horse's ear, and call out to him how he is to go." "Well," answered the man, "for once we will try it."

When the time came, the mother harnessed the horse, and placed Thumbling in its ear, and then the little creature cried "Gee up, gee up!"

Then it went quite properly as if with its master, and the cart went the right way into the forest. It so happened that just as he was turning a corner, and the little one was crying "Gee up," two strange men came towards him. "My word!" said one of them. "What is this? There is a cart coming, and a driver is calling to the horse, and still he is not to be seen!" "That can't be right," said the other, "we will follow the cart and see where it stops." The cart, however, drove right into the forest, and exactly to the place where the wood had been cut. When Thumbling saw his father, he cried to him, "Seest thou, father, here I am with the cart; now take me down." The father got hold of the horse with his left hand, and with the right took his little son out of the ear. Thumbling sat down quite merrily on a straw, but when the two strange men saw him, they did not know what to say for astonishment. Then one of them took the other aside and said,

"Hark, the little fellow would make our fortune if we exhibited him in a large town, for money. We will buy him." They went to the peasant and said, "Sell us the little man. He shall be well treated with us." "No," replied the father, "he is the apple of my eye, and all the money in the world cannot buy him from me." Thumbling, however, when he heard of the bargain, had crept up the folds of his father's coat, placed himself on his shoulder, and whispered in his ear, "Father, do give me away, I will soon come back again." Then the father parted with him to the two men for a handsome bit of money. "Where wilt thou sit?" they said to him. "Oh, just set me on the rim of your hat, and then I can walk backwards and forwards and look at the country, and still not fall down." They did as he wished, and when Thumbling had taken leave of his father, they went away with him. They walked until it was dusk, and then the little fellow said, "Do take me down, I want to come down." The man took his hat off, and put the little fellow on the ground by the wayside, and he leapt and crept about a little between the sods, and then he suddenly slipped into a mouse-hole which he had sought out. "Good evening, gentlemen, just go home without me," he cried to them, and mocked them. They ran thither and stuck their sticks into the mouse-hole, but it was all lost labour. Thumbling crept still farther in, and as it soon became quite dark, they were forced to go home with their vexation and their empty purses.

When Thumbling saw that they were gone, he crept back out of the subterranean passage. "It is so dangerous to walk on the ground in the dark," said he; "how easily a neck or leg is broken!" Fortunately he knocked against an empty snail-shell. "Thank God!" said he. "In that I can pass the night in safety," and got into it. Not long afterwards, when he was just going to sleep, he heard two men go by, and one of them was saying, "How shall we contrive to get hold of the rich pastor's silver and gold?" "I could tell thee that," cried Thumbling, interrupting them. "What was that?" said one of the thieves in a fright, "I heard some one speaking." They stood still listening, and Thumbling spoke again, and said, "Take me with you, and I'll help you."

"But where art thou?" "Just look on the ground, and observe from whence my voice comes," he replied. There the thieves at length found him, and lifted him up. "Thou little imp, how wilt thou help us?" they said. "A great deal," said he, "I will creep into the pastor's room through the iron bars, and will reach out to you whatever you want to have." "Come then," they said, "and we will see what thou canst do." When they got to the pastor's house, Thumbling crept into the room, but instantly cried out with all his might, "Do you want to have everything that is here?" The thieves were alarmed, and said, "But do speak softly, so as not to waken any one!" Thumbling, however, behaved as if he had not understood this, and cried again, "What do you want? Do you want to have everything that is here?" The cook, who slept in the next room, heard this and sat up in bed, and listened. The thieves, however, had in their fright run some distance away, but at last they took courage, and thought, "The little rascal wants to mock us." They came back and whispered to him, "Come, be serious, and reach something out to us." Then Thumbling again cried as loudly as he could, "I really will give you everything, only put your hands in." The maid who was listening, heard this quite distinctly, and jumped out of bed and rushed to the door. The thieves took flight, and ran as if the Wild Huntsman were behind them, but as the maid could not see anything, she went to strike a light. When she came to the place with it, Thumbling, unperceived, betook himself to the granary, and the maid, after she had examined every corner and found nothing, lay down in her bed again, and believed that, after all, she had only been dreaming with open eyes and ears.

Thumbling had climbed up among the hay and found a beautiful place to sleep in; there he intended to rest until day, and then go home again to his parents. But he had other things to go through. Truly there is much affliction and misery in this world! When day dawned, the maid arose from her bed to feed the cows. Her first walk was into the barn, where she laid hold of an armful of hay, and precisely that very one in which poor Thumbling was lying asleep. He, however, was sleeping so soundly that he was aware of nothing, and did not awake until he was in the mouth of the cow, who had picked him up with the hay. "Ah, heavens!" cried he, "how have I got into the fulling mill?" but he soon discovered where he was. Then it was necessary to be careful not to let himself go between the teeth and be dismembered, but he was nevertheless forced to slip down into the stomach with the hay. "In this little room the windows are forgotten," said he, "and no sun shines in, neither will a candle be brought." His quarters were especially unpleasing to him, and the worst was, more and more hay was always coming in by the door, and the space grew less and less. Then, at length in his anguish, he cried as loud as he could, "Bring me no more fodder, bring me no more fodder." The maid was just milking the cow, and when she heard some one speaking, and saw no one, and perceived that it was the same voice that she had heard in the night, she was so terrified that she slipped off her stool, and spilt the milk. She ran in the greatest haste to her master, and said, "Oh, heavens, pastor, the cow has been speaking!" "Thou art mad," replied the pastor; but he went himself to the byre to see what

Thumbling

was there. Hardly, however, had he set his foot inside than Thumbling again cried, "Bring me no more fodder, bring me no more fodder." Then the pastor himself was alarmed, and thought that an evil spirit had gone into the cow, and ordered her to be killed. She was killed, but the stomach, in which Thumbling was, was thrown on the midden. Thumbling had great difficulty in working his way; however, he succeeded so far as to get some room, but, just as he was going to thrust his head out, a new misfortune occurred. A hungry wolf ran thither, and swallowed the whole stomach at one gulp. Thumbling did not lose courage. "Perhaps," thought he, "the wolf will listen to what I have got to say," and he called to him from out of his stomach, "Dear wolf, I know of a magnificent feast for thee."

"Where is it to be had?" said the wolf.

"In such and such a house; thou must creep into it through the kitchen-sink, and wilt find cakes, and bacon, and sausages, and as much of them as thou canst eat," and he described to him exactly his father's house. The wolf did not require to be told this twice, squeezed himself in at night through the sink, and ate to his heart's content in the larder. When he had eaten his fill, he wanted to go out again, but he had become so big that he could not go out by the same way. Thumbling had reckoned on this, and now began to make a violent noise in the wolf's body, and raged and screamed as loudly as he could. "Wilt thou be quiet," said the wolf, "thou wilt waken up the people!" "Eh, what," replied the little fellow, "thou hast eaten thy fill, and I will make merry likewise," and began once more to scream with all his strength. At last his father and mother were aroused by it, and ran to the room and looked in through the opening in the door. When they saw that a wolf was inside, they ran away, and the husband fetched his axe, and the wife the scythe. "Stay behind," said the man, when they entered the room. "When I have given him a blow, if he is not killed by it, thou must cut him down and hew his body to pieces." Then Thumbling heard his parents' voices, and cried, "Dear father, I am here; I am in the wolf's body." Said the father, full of joy, "Thank God, our dear child has found us again," and bade the woman take away her scythe, that Thumbling might not be hurt with it. After that he raised his arm, and struck the wolf such a blow on his head that he fell down dead, and then they got knives and scissors and cut his body open, and drew the little fellow forth. "Ah," said the father, "what sorrow we have gone through for thy sake." "Yes, father, I have gone about the world a great deal. Thank heaven, I breathe fresh air again!" "Where hast thou been, then?" "Ah, father, I have been in a mouse's hole, in a cow's stomach, and then in a wolf's; now I will stay with you." "And we will not sell thee again, no, not for all the riches in the world," said his parents, and they embraced and kissed their dear Thumbling. They gave him to eat and to drink, and had some new clothes made for him, for his own had been spoiled on his journey.

Thumbling's Travels

A German tale from the Brothers Grimm

*I*n this second variation of a thumbling adventure, the Brothers Grimm depict a much more independent, daring, and devilish thumbling.

In "Thumbling's Travels," Thumbling actually seeks out adventure. His travels take him to a king's treasure-chamber, where once again he is involved in a crime, but this time with reward.

A certain tailor had a son, who happened to be small, and no bigger than a Thumb, and on this account he was always called Thumbling. He had, however, some courage in him, and said to his father, "Father, I must and will go out into the world." "That's right, my son," said the old man, and took a long darning-needle and made a knob of sealing-wax on it at the candle, "and there is a sword for thee to take with thee on the way." Then the little tailor wanted to have one more meal with them, and hopped into the kitchen to see what his lady mother had cooked for the last time. It was, however, just dished up, and the dish stood on the hearth. Then he said, "Mother, what is there to eat to-day?" "See for thyself," said his mother. So Thumbling jumped on to the hearth, and peeped into the dish, but as he stretched his neck in too far the steam from the food caught hold of him, and carried him up the chimney. He rode about in the air on the steam for a while, until at length he sank down to the ground again. Now the little tailor was outside in the wide world, and he travelled about, and went to a master in his craft, but the food was not good enough for him. "Mistress, if you give us no better food," said Thumbling, "I will go away, and early tomorrow morning I will write with chalk on the door of your house, 'Too many potatoes, too little meat! Farewell, Mr. Potato-King.'" "What wouldst thou have forsooth, grasshopper?" said the mistress, and grew angry, and seized a dish-cloth, and was just going to strike him; but my little tailor crept nimbly under a thimble, peeped out from beneath it, and put his tongue out at the mistress. She took up the thimble, and wanted to get hold of him, but little Thumbling hopped into the cloth, and while the mistress was opening it out and looking for him, he got into a crevice in the table. "Ho, ho, lady mistress," cried he, and thrust his head out, and when she began to strike him he leapt down into the drawer. At last, however, she caught him and drove him out of the house.

The little tailor journeyed on and came to a great forest, and there he fell in with a band of robbers who had a design to steal the King's treasure. When they saw the little tailor, they thought, "A little fellow like that can creep through a key-hole and serve as picklock to us." "Hollo," cried one of them, "thou giant Goliath, wilt thou go to the treasure-chamber with us? Thou canst slip thyself in and throw out the money."

Thumbling reflected a while, and at length he said "yes," and went with them to the treasure-chamber. Then he looked at the doors above and below, to see if there was any crack in them. It was not long before he espied one which was broad enough to let him in. He was therefore about to get in at once, but one of the two sentries who stood before the door observed him, and said to the other, "What an ugly spider is creeping there; I will kill it." "Let the poor creature alone," said the other, "it has done thee no harm." Then Thumbling got safely through the crevice into the treasure-chamber, opened the window beneath which the robbers were standing, and threw out to them one thaler after another. When the little tailor was in the full swing of his work, he heard the King coming to inspect his treasure-chamber, and crept hastily into a hiding-place. The King noticed that several solid thalers were missing, but could not conceive who could have stolen them, for locks and bolts were in good condition, and all seemed well guarded. Then he went away again, and said to the sentries, "Be on the watch, some one is after the money." When therefore Thumbling recommenced his labours, they heard the money moving, and a sound of klink, klink, klink. They ran swiftly in to seize the thief, but the little tailor, who heard them coming, was still swifter, and leapt into a corner and covered himself with a thaler, so that nothing could be seen of him, and at the same time he mocked the sentries and cried, "Here am I!" The sentries ran thither, but as they got there, he had already hopped into another corner under a thaler, and was crying, "Ho, ho, here am I!" The watchmen sprang there in haste, but Thumbling had long ago got into a third corner, and was crying, "Ho, ho, here am I!" And thus he made fools of them, and drove them so long round about the treasure-chamber that they were weary and went away. Then by degrees he threw all the thalers out, despatching the last with all his might, then hopped nimbly upon it, and flew down with it through the window. The robbers paid him great compliments. "Thou art a valiant hero," said they; "wilt thou be our captain?"

Thumbling, however, declined, and said he wanted to see the world first. They now divided the booty, but the little tailor only asked for a kreuzer because he could not carry more.

Then he once more buckled on his sword, bade the robbers good-bye, and took to the road. First, he went to work with some masters, but he had no liking for that, and at last he hired himself as man-servant in an inn. The maids, however, could not endure him, for he saw all that they did secretly, without their seeing him, and he told their master and mistress what they had taken off the plates, and carried away out of the cellar, for themselves. Then said they, "Wait, and we will pay thee off!" and arranged with each other to play him a trick. Soon afterwards when one of the maids was mowing in the garden, and saw Thumbling jumping about and creeping up and down the plants, she mowed him up quickly with the grass, tied all in a great cloth, and secretly threw it to the cows. Now amongst them there was a great black one, who swallowed him down with it without hurting him. Down below, however, it pleased him ill, for it was quite dark, neither was any candle burning. When the cow was being milked he cried,

> "Strip, strap, strull,
> Will the pail soon be full?"

But the noise of the milking prevented his being understood. After this the master of the house came into the cow-byre and said, "That cow shall be killed to-morrow." Then Thumbling was so alarmed that he cried out in a clear voice, "Let me out first, for I am shut up inside her." The master heard that quite well, but did not know from whence the voice came. "Where art thou?" asked he. "In the black one," answered Thumbling, but the master did not understand what that meant, and went out.

Next morning the cow was killed. Happily Thumbling did not meet with one blow at the cutting up and chopping; he got among the sausage-meat. And when the butcher came in and began his work, he cried out with all his might, "Don't chop too deep, don't chop too deep, I am amongst it." No one heard this because of the noise of the chopping-knife. Now poor Thumbling was in trouble, but trouble sharpens the wits, and he sprang out so adroitly between the blows that none of them touched him, and he got out with a whole skin. But still he could not get away, there was nothing for it, and he had to let himself be thrust into a black-pudding with the bits of bacon. His quarters there were rather confined, and besides that he was hung up in the chimney to be smoked, and there time did hang terribly heavy on his hands.

At length in winter he was taken down again, as the black-pudding had to be set before a guest. When the hostess was cutting it in slices, he took care not to stretch out his head too far lest a bit of it should be cut off; at last he saw his opportunity, cleared a passage for himself, and jumped out.

The little tailor, however, would not stay any longer in a house where he fared so ill, but at once set out on his journey again. But his liberty did not last long. In the open country he met with a fox who snapped him up in a fit of absence. "Hollo, Mr. Fox," cried the little tailor, "it is I who am sticking in your throat, set me at liberty again."

"Thou art right," answered the fox. "Thou art next to nothing for me, but if thou wilt promise me the fowls in thy father's yard I will let thee go." "With all my heart," replied Thumbling. "Thou shalt have all the cocks and hens, that I promise thee." Then the fox let him go again, and himself carried him home. When the father once more saw his dear son, he willingly gave the fox all the fowls which he had. "For this I likewise bring thee a handsome bit of money," said Thumbling, and gave his father the kreuzer which he had earned on his travels.

"But why did the fox get the poor chickens to eat?" "Oh, you goose, your father would surely love his child far more than the fowls in the yard!"

Lipuniushka

A tale from Russia

*I*n this brief thumbling tale Lipuniushka plays a trick on the rich barin [baron]. This Russian variation of a thumbling tale has interesting ethnic touches, like the blini pancake and Lipuniushka's birth from a fluff of spinning cotton.

As you read, note the similarities in plot between this tale and the Brothers Grimm tale of "Thumbling"; for example, the thumbling encourages his father to sell him with the promise that he will escape and return home. Unlike the Grimm tale, however, this story ends rather abruptly.

Once upon a time there was an old lady and an old man who didn't have any children of their own. One day the old man went to the field to plough. The old lady stayed home to make blini.

After the old woman had cooked the pancakes, she said, "If only we had a son, he would bring these blini to his father. But who will take them to him, as it is now?"

Suddenly a tiny, tiny boy crawled out of a fluff of cotton. He said, "Hello, Mother!"

The old lady asked, "Where are you from, sonny, and what is your name?"

The little boy replied, "Do you remember the cotton you were spinning into thread and winding around the spool, Mother? That's where I came from. My name is Lipuniushka. Give me the blini, and I will take them to Father."

The old woman said, "Will you be able to carry them all by yourself, Lipuniushka?"

"I will."

The old woman tied the pancakes in a bundle and gave them to her new little son. Lipuniushka took the bundle and ran to the field.

On his way to the field he came across a little tuft of grass in the road.

He cried out, "Father, Father, lift me over this tuft of grass. I have brought you some blini."

The old man in the field heard a small voice calling and went to see who it was.

He lifted the tiny boy over the tuft of grass and asked, "Where are you from, sonny?"

The little boy replied, "I came out of a cotton fluff, Father," and he gave him the pancakes.

When the old man sat down to eat his lunch, the little boy said, "Let me plough the field, Father."

"You don't have enough strength to plough," the old man replied.

But Lipuniushka grabbed the wooden plough and began to plough the field, singing as he worked.

Now, a rich barin was riding by the field at the time. He saw the old man eating his lunch while the horse seemed to be ploughing by itself.

The barin jumped out of his coach and asked the old man, "How is it possible for your horse to plough the field by itself?"

"The horse isn't ploughing by itself," the old man answered. "That's my little boy who is ploughing and singing."

The barin came closer and heard the singing. He saw Lipuniushka.

"Old man, sell me your little boy," he said.

The old man replied, "No, I can't sell him. He is my only child."

Fearing that the old man would be in trouble if he refused to obey, Lipuniushka went over to him and whispered, "Sell me, Father, and I will run away from the gentleman afterwards."

So the old man sold the little boy for one hundred rubles. After paying the money, the barin wrapped the little boy up in a handkerchief and put him into his pocket.

He rode home and told his wife, "I have brought you an interesting plaything."

"Show me," his wife said.

The barin took the handkerchief out of his pocket and unrolled it, but there was nothing there. Lipuniushka had long ago run home to his father.

Pouçot

A tale from France

This brief French tale is a twentieth-century example of Tom Thumb's survival in oral tradition. It was collected in 1960 from Mme. Bellion, age 65, of Bretignolles. While brief, it has a certain charm, although this is one of those tales in which a thumbling, after being eaten by an animal, must endure the indignity of traveling through the animal's digestive system to come out at the other end. Note that this is a French version of the tale we know in English as "Tom Thumb." The French "Petit Poucet" (see page 47 in this collection) is a quite different tale.

T om Thumb was so very very small that he could turn up anywhere.

One day he went to his aunt's house. As she wasn't there, he climbed into the cheese basket. In those days it was hung from a beam in a storeroom. He tasted several of the cheeses, and then he ate the best ones. After that, he hid in the straw under them.

When his aunt came back she brought down the basket to take out the cheeses.

"Oh," she said, "who has been tasting my cheeses?" Tom Thumb, who was in the straw in the basket, kept quiet.

Off went the aunt to the cow barn. She put the straw from the basket into the manger. At that moment Tom Thumb's uncle came along. He put a cabbage on top of the straw in the manger. Tom Thumb hid in the leaves. The cow ate a leaf and swallowed Tom Thumb whole.

Then the aunt came in to milk the cow, and what should she hear but the cow talking!

"What on earth am I doing in here!" shouted Tom Thumb (imprisoned in the cow's belly).

The aunt was afraid. "Is this cow under a spell?"

Whereupon the cow raised a leg and pushed the aunt over.

"All is lost!" cried the aunt.

The cow wanted to [poop]. She produced Tom Thumb in a cowpat, and as there was a bucket of water quite close, he jumped in and washed himself.

In the end the aunt believed that the cow was under a spell good and proper, and she told everyone about it.

Hasan, the Heroic Mouse-Child

A tale from Turkey

This charming little tale would work well told aloud. It is easy to learn, with several delightful sounds for the teller to play with... "Deh," "Chush," and "Clink." This is the basic thumbling-takes-lunch-to-father-and-tricks-robbers tale, but the thumbling here is portrayed as a mouse!

However, once again, the thumbling makes up in resourcefulness for what he lacks in size. As Hasan concludes after a successful venture in which he obtains gold coins for his parents, "Even a mouse-child can make himself tall enough to help his parents."

Once there was and once there wasn't a man who had no child. Oh, he and his wife *wanted* a child, but none came. At last his wife prayed, "O Allah, send us a child, even if it be no bigger nor better than a mouse."

That day, the ears of Allah were open, and in good time the woman gave birth to a child. Nothing but a mouse he was, small and gray, with wise eyes and twitching whiskers. The neighbors were surprised, but the man and his wife were glad to have any child at all, and they named him Hasan.

As the child grew, he helped more and more around the house, and his parents rejoiced in their lively son.

One morning as the good woman was preparing a hot lunch for her husband, Hasan stood up tall on a stool. "See how big I am, my mother," he said. "Let me take the lunch to my father in the field."

"You *are* big, my dear," answered his mother, "but you are not quite big enough to manage our donkey while he carries the lunch to the field."

"Listen, my mother," said Hasan. "I can say '*Deh*' and '*Chush*' as well as the rest, and the donkey knows me well. If I am high on his back, the donkey will go and stop for me. I can ride in the saddlebag. You'll see!"

So Hasan's mother put the lunch in a tin box and tucked it into one pocket of the saddlebag, and she helped Hasan into the other pocket.

"*Deh!*" called the mouse-child, and off the donkey started for the field.

Hasan's father was surprised to see the donkey coming all by himself to the field. "*Aman!*" he exclaimed. But just as he was about to take to his heels with fear, "*Chush!*" shouted Hasan. And there stood Hasan, peeking over the edge of the saddlebag, with his bright eyes watching his father's surprise.

His father laughed and helped him down, and the two ate a good hot lunch together.

When it was time for his father to work again, the mouse-child scrambled up into the saddlebag. "*Deh!*" he shouted, and off went the donkey toward home.

On their way home, they came to the village fountain. "*Chush!*" shouted Hasan, and the donkey stopped. "You must be thirsty, my donkey," said the mouse-child. "Have a good drink while I climb to the top of that poplar tree. If I'm up high, I can see how the whole village looks!"

Leg over leg, Hasan climbed to the top of the tree. "Ah! Indeed I *can* see the whole village!" he said to himself.

Suddenly Hasan saw three men behind a bush near the fountain. They were counting: "One, two, three, one, two, three, one, two, three." And they were counting *gold coins*!

"Hmmnn!" said Hasan. "If they are hiding behind that bush, those may be stolen coins. I'll soon find out."

And boldly Hasan began to whistle the tune the village watchman whistled as he came down the street.

Startled, the three men looked this way and that, but they could not see the watchman. Frightened, they shoved the sack of gold coins into a hole under the bush. Then they ran out of the village as fast as they could go.

As soon as they had gone, Hasan scrambled down the poplar tree. "I can't lift that sack, but I *can* lift those coins one by one," he said.

And, one by one, Hasan carried the coins to the saddlebag of the donkey and dropped them, *Clink! Clink! Clink!*, into the pocket.

As soon as all of the coins were safe in the saddlebag, Hasan pushed the empty sack down deep, deep, deep, in that hole under the bush.

Then, climbing into the other pocket of the saddlebag, Hasan shouted *"Deh!"* and off the donkey trotted toward home.

"Chush!" called Hasan as the donkey came to Hasan's house, and the donkey stopped. Hasan's mother came to the door.

"Hasan!" she said. "I was afraid you were lost!"

Hasan laughed. "No, Mother. I was not lost. But I found something very useful. Come and see!" And he scrambled over to the other pocket of the saddlebag.

When his mother saw the gold coins, she could scarcely believe her eyes. And she was even more surprised when Hasan told her how he had frightened the robbers. "My mother," said Hasan, "even a mouse-child can make himself tall enough to help his parents."

It wasn't long before the man and his wife and the mouse-child were living in a fine new house. And, just for Hasan the hero, the house had a little balcony on top, so that Hasan could watch all the people come and go.

You see, you never can tell what will happen when you ask for a child no bigger nor better than a mouse!

Loudmouth Thummas

A tale from Slovenia

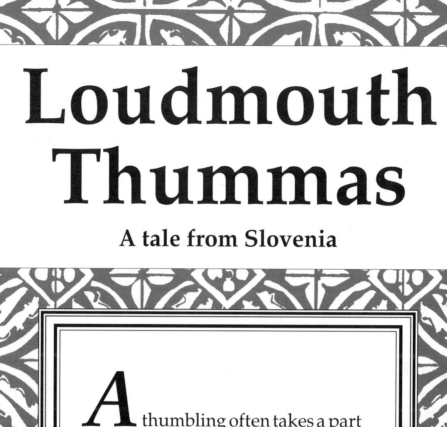

A thumbling often takes a part in the tale of a trickster who teams up with robbers only to raise a ruckus and rout them. This version is a bit unusual in that it ends poorly for the thumbling. But both he (and the reader) learn the valuable lesson that it isn't wise to hang out with robbers unless you want to be robbed.

I have retold this in a "tellable" format, which should make it useful for storytellers. The tale's repeated episodes and the lively banter between the loudmouthed little boy and the robbers make this an especially enjoyable story to tell.

*O*nce there was a woman who wanted a child so badly.

She said, "Oh I would love a little son . . . even if he were no bigger than my thumb!"

And do you know, she got her wish.

A tiny son was born to this woman.

But he was no bigger than her thumb!

And though they fed him and cared for him tenderly,

the child never grew beyond that size.

So they called him "Little Thummas."

By the time Thummas was twelve,

he was bored with life in a country village.

"Time to go out into the wide world!" said Thummas.

So his mother made him a little packet of food for the journey and Thummas set off.

What a hard journey it was.

If he was blocked by a stone it seemed a huge boulder to Thummas.

He would try to go around . . .

but if there were several stones together . . .

Thummas would have to hoist himself up and over those boulders.

And if he fell into a rut in the road . . .

he had such a time trying to climb out again.

However by evening he had made his way out of the village and reached the forest.

Thummas was enchanted by the forest.

He climbed over logs.

He crept under ferns.

He clung to the mossy sides of boulders to pull himself to the top and then slid down
   the other side, bouncing on the soft green moss.

And when darkness fell Thummas curled up under a large mushroom, dry and cozy
   as could be.

Now in that forest lived three robbers.

When it was dark, the three robbers set off to do their dirty work in the village.

Tromping through the forest in the darkness they could not see Thummas curled up
   on the forest floor.

"WHOMP!" The first robber tripped over Thummas.

Thummas sat right up.
"HEY! Watch where you're WALKING!"

The robber looked around.
He couldn't *see* anyone.

The second robber was following behind the first...
"WHOMP!"
He tripped over Thummas.

"WILL you watch where you are stepping, you big LUMMOX!" hollered Thummas.

The robber *looked*
but he didn't *see* anyone.

Following behind, came the third robber...
"WHOMP!"

Thummas jumped up and began to shake his fists at those huge robbers.
"What is the MATTER with you BIG LUMPS?
Can't you watch where you are WALKING?"

The three robbers came back and peered down.
There was a little boy, no bigger than a thumb.
He was jumping up and down in anger and shouting at them.
"Watch where you WALK
you big LUMMOXES!"

A boy?
Three inches high?
This could be of some use to *robbers*!

"Hi there, son.
What is your name?"
"Thummas I am!

Thummas I be!
I may not be tall
But I'm smarter than THEE!"

And that silly boy began to chortle at his cleverness.

"Well, Clever Thummas,
we'll just take you with us.
A tiny thing like you might come in handy in our line of work."

The first robber plucked Thummas from the ground and set him onto his shoulder.

"Well," thought Thummas, "I wanted adventure.
But I never thought I'd end up in the company of *robbers*!"

Soon the robbers reached a farm.
"There's a white horse in this stable and we plan to steal it," said the first robber.
"Now, Thummas, since you are so clever,
just roll under the stable door . . .
climb up and undo the latch . . .
so we can come in and steal that horse."
And he set Thummas on the ground by the stable door.

Easy enough.
Thummas laid himself down and *rolled* right under the stable door.
But once he was inside, he decided to have some fun with those robbers instead of
   obeying their orders.
"Now climb up and undo the latch," whispered the robbers,
and they waited for the door to open.
Instead they heard the *loudest* voice hollering from inside the stable.
"WHICH HORSE DO YOU WANT ME TO STEAL?
IS IT THE BLACK ONE OR THE WHITE ONE?"
"Shhhh! Shhhh!"
The robbers tried to hush Thummas.
"The farmer will hear you!"

But Thummas would not shut up.
"WHICH HORSE DO YOU WANT ME TO STEAL?
IS IT THE BLACK ONE OR THE WHITE ONE?"

"Shhhh! Shhhh!"
But it was too late.
Here came the farmer at a run.
The robbers jumped to hide in the bushes.
The farmer unlocked the stable door and rushed inside waving his lantern.
By this time clever Thummas had crawled up and hidden himself in the white horse's
    mane.
"Put out that LIGHT!" bellowed Thummas.
The farmer saw no one in the stable.
Yet he could clearly hear a loud voice.
He shined his light at the white horse.
"GET THAT LIGHT OUT OF MY EYES!" hollered the hidden Thummas.
And the farmer, thinking his horse was talking,
threw the lantern into the air,
ran back into his house,
and locked the door.

The three robbers came out of their hiding places and led the white horse away,
with Thummas still clinging to its mane.

At the next farmhouse, the robbers planned to steal a big tub of butter.
That farmer's wife was known for her fine cream and butter.
They put Thummas in at the pantry window.
"Just climb down and unlock the door," said the robbers.
"We will do the rest."

Inside the pantry, Thummas saw two tubs of butter,
a big tub and a little tub.
Thummas could not resist.

"WHICH ONE DO YOU WANT?
THE BIG ONE OR THE LITTLE ONE?"

"Shhhh! Shhhh!
You'll wake the farmer's wife!"

"WHICH ONE DO YOU WANT?
THE BIG ONE OR THE LITTLE ONE?"

"Shhhh! Shhhh!"

But it was too late.
Here came the farmer's wife at a run.
Straight into the pantry she ran, and grabbed up her large butter
   tub . . . .
But Thummas, who was sitting inside the tub, hollered out,
"PUT ME DOWN, OLD WOMAN!"

"AAAH!" she dropped the tub and ran for the house.
"My butter is bewitched!
It TALKED to me!"

So the robbers came in and took up the tub of butter and went on their way;
Thummas was still sitting in the butter tub.
It was now getting late.
But before the robbers went back to their forest hideout, they decided to steal a bit of
   meat from the butcher shop.

"Thummas," they said,
"Just slide down the chimney,
unlock the door,
and we will do the rest."

So Thummas slid down the chimney.
Inside he saw piles of meat on one side of the room
and piles of skins on the other side.

"WHICH DO YOU WANT ME TO STEAL?
THE MEAT OR THE SKINS?"
hollered Thummas.

"Shhhh! Shhhh!"
"The butcher sleeps over the shop.
He will hear you!"

"WHICH DO YOU WANT ME TO STEAL?
THE MEAT OR THE SKINS?"

"Shhhh! Shhhh!"
But it was too late.
Here came the butcher,
waving his butcher knife and bellowing,
"Where is that ROBBER?"

But Thummas, hiding under the skins, called out
"PUT THAT BUTCHER KNIFE AWAY!
CAN'T YOU SEE WE'RE SKINNED ALREADY?"

The butcher thought his skins were talking to him.
"AAACK!"
He dropped the knife and ran out of the shop.
He ran back upstairs, and buried his head in his bed.

So the robbers came in and helped themselves to the meat.

They loaded it all on the white horse,
tucked Thummas into the butter tub,
and trudged back to their forest camp.

There the robbers cooked up a supper of meat roasted in butter.
And when it was done they began to gnaw and tear at the delicious roasted meat.

But not a scrap did they give to little Thummas.
"HEY! What about ME!
I did all the WORK.

Where's MY supper!"

The huge robbers just laughed.
"Get out of here, runt.
We're done with you NOW.

You expect us to SHARE?
You're too small to MAKE us do anything."

And they turned back to their food, ignoring poor Thummas.

He was furious.
Thummas climbed up on the roof of the robbers' shack.
He began to jump around, hollering as loudly as he could.
"GIVE ME SOME STOLEN MEAT! GIVE ME SOME STOLEN MEAT!"
But this time they were deep in the forest.
No one heard to come to Thummas's aid.

The robbers laughed and calling out
"Which do you want . . .
the skins or the BONES? . . ."
they tossed a huge bone up onto the roof.

Poor Thummas was knocked over by the bone and fell from the roof.
Sadly he picked himself up, bruised and sore, and started his long walk back home.

"Well, I learned one thing," thought Thummas.
"If you hang out with robbers.
You'll probably get ROBBED!"

The Hazel-nut Child

A tale from Bukovina

*I*n this tale our little thumbling, "no bigger than a hazel-nut," ties himself to a stork and is carried off to Africa for the winter. The King there is so fond of him that the Hazel-nut child comes home with a fine reward.

"The Hazel-nut Child" is a Bukovinian tale. Bukovina is a region in the foothills of the Eastern Carpathian Mountains, located on the border between Romania and the Ukraine.

*T*here was once upon a time a couple who had no children, and they prayed Heaven every day to send them a child, though it were no bigger than a hazel-nut. At last Heaven heard their prayer and sent them a child exactly the size of a hazel-nut, and it never grew an inch. The parents were very devoted to the little creature, and nursed and tended it carefully. Their tiny son too was as clever as he could be, and so sharp and sensible that all the neighbours marvelled over the wise things he said and did.

When the Hazel-nut child was fifteen years old, and was sitting one day in an egg-shell on the table beside his mother, she turned to him and said, "You are now fifteen years old, and nothing can be done with you. What do you intend to be?"

"A messenger," answered the Hazel-nut child.

Then his mother burst out laughing and said, "What an idea! You a messenger! Why, your little feet would take an hour to go the distance an ordinary person could do in a minute!"

But the Hazel-nut child replied, "Nevertheless I mean to be a messenger! Just send me a message and you'll see that I shall be back in next to no time."

So his mother said, "Very well, go to your aunt in the neighbouring village, and fetch me a comb." The Hazel-nut child jumped quickly out of the egg-shell and ran out into the street. Here he found a man on horseback who was just setting out for the neighbouring village. He crept up the horse's leg, sat down under the saddle, and then began to pinch the horse and to prick it with a pin. The horse plunged and reared and then set off at a hard gallop, which it continued in spite of its rider's efforts to stop it. When they reached the village, the Hazel-nut child left off pricking the horse, and the poor tired creature pursued its way at a snail's pace. The Hazel-nut child took advantage of this, and crept down the horse's leg; then he ran to his aunt and asked her for a comb. On the way home he met another rider, and did the return journey in exactly the same way. When he handed his mother the comb that his aunt had given him, she was much amazed and asked him, "But how did you manage to get back so quickly?"

"Ah! mother," he replied, "you see I was quite right when I said I knew a messenger was the profession for me."

His father too possessed a horse which he often used to take out into the fields to graze. One day he took the Hazel-nut child with him. At midday the father turned to his small son and said, "Stay here and look after the horse. I must go home and give your mother a message, but I shall be back soon."

When his father had gone, a robber passed by and saw the horse grazing without anyone watching it, for of course he could not see the Hazel-nut child hidden in the grass. So he mounted the horse and rode away. But the Hazel-nut child, who was the most active little creature, climbed up the horse's tail and began to bite it on the back, enraging the creature to such an extent that it paid no attention to the direction the robber tried to make it go in, but galloped straight home. The father was much astonished when he saw a stranger riding his horse, but the Hazel-nut child climbed down quickly and told him all that had happened, and his father had the robber arrested at once and put into prison.

One autumn when the Hazel-nut child was 20 years old he said to his parents: "Farewell, my dear father and mother. I am going to set out into the world, and as soon as I have become rich I will return home to you."

The parents laughed at the little man's words, but did not believe him for a moment. In the evening the Hazel-nut child crept on to the roof, where some storks had built their nest. The storks were fast asleep, and he climbed on to the back of the father-stork and bound a silk cord round the joint of one of its wings, then he crept among its soft downy feathers and fell asleep.

The next morning the storks flew towards the south, for winter was approaching. The Hazel-nut child flew through the air on the stork's back, and when he wanted to rest he bound his silk cord on to the joint of the bird's other wing, so that it could not fly any farther. In this way he reached the country of the black people, where the storks  took up their abode close to the capital. When the people saw the Hazel-nut child they were much astonished, and took him with the stork to the King of the country. The King was delighted with the little creature and kept him always beside him, and he soon grew so fond of the little man that he gave him a diamond four times as big as himself. The Hazel-nut child fastened the diamond firmly under the stork's neck with a ribbon, and when he saw that the other storks were getting ready for their northern flight, he untied the silk cord from his stork's wings, and away they went, getting nearer home every minute. At length the Hazel-nut child came to his native village; then he undid

The Hazel-nut Child

the ribbon from the stork's neck and the diamond fell to the ground; he covered it first with sand and stones, and then ran to get his parents, so that they might carry the treasure home, for he himself was not able to lift the great diamond.

So the Hazel-nut child and his parents lived in happiness and prosperity after this till they died.

Thumbikin

A tale from Norway

*H*ere, from the nineteenth-century collection of Peter Asbjörnsen and Jörgen Moe, is the story of a sassy thumbling who pushes his luck just a little too far and ends up paying a high price for his daring.

With this story, the thumbling's world continues to expand, this time with a venture into marriage. But despite his grown-up adventure, he still can't help reverting to his childish ways, tormenting his mother with his hide-and-seek games and letting his greed get the better of him.

*O*nce on a time there was a woman who had an only son, and he was no taller than your thumb; and so they called him Thumbikin.

Now, when he had come to be old enough to know right and wrong, his mother told him to go out and woo him a bride, for now she said it was high time he thought about getting a wife. When Thumbikin heard that, he was very glad; so they got their driving gear in order and set off, and his mother put him into her bosom. Now they were going to a palace where there was such an awfully big Princess, but when they had gone a bit of the way, Thumbikin was lost and gone. His mother hunted for him everywhere, and bawled to him, and wept because he was lost, and she couldn't find him again.

"Pip, pip," said Thumbikin, "here I am," and he had hidden himself in the horse's mane.

So he came out, and had to give his word to his mother that he wouldn't do so any more. But when they had driven a bit farther on, Thumbikin was lost again. His mother hunted for him, and called him and wept; but gone he was, and gone he stayed.

"Pip, pip," said Thumbikin at last; and then she heard how he laughed and tittered, but she couldn't find him at all for the life of her.

"Pip, pip, why, here I am now!" said Thumbikin, and came out of the horse's ear.

So he had to give his word that he wouldn't hide himself again; but they had scarce driven a bit farther before he was gone again. He couldn't help it. As for his mother, she hunted, and wept, and called him by name; but gone he was, and gone he stayed; and the more she hunted, the less she could find him in any way.

"Pip, pip, here I am then," said Thumbikin.

But she couldn't make out at all where he was, his voice sounded so dull and muffled.

So she hunted, and he kept on saying, "Pip, here I am," and laughed and chuckled that she couldn't find him; but all at once the horse snorted, and it snorted Thumbikin out, for he had crept up one of his nostrils.

Then his mother took him and put him into a bag; she knew no other way, for she saw well enough he couldn't help hiding himself.

So when they came to the palace the match was soon made, for the Princess thought him a pretty little chap, and it wasn't long before the wedding came on too.

Now, when they were going to sit down to the wedding-feast, Thumbikin sat at the table by the Princess's side; but he had worse than no seat, for when he was to eat he couldn't reach up to the table; and so, if the Princess hadn't helped him up on to it, he wouldn't have got a bit to eat.

Now it went good and well so long as he had to eat off a plate, but then there came a great bowl of porridge—that he couldn't reach up to; but Thumbikin soon found out a way to help himself; he climbed up and sat on the lip of the bowl. But then there was a pat of melting butter right in the middle of the bowl, and that he couldn't reach to dip his porridge into it, and so he went on and took his seat at the edge of the melting butter; but just then who should come but the Princess, with a great spoonful of porridge to dip it into the butter; and, alas! she went too near to Thumbikin, and tipped him over; and so he fell over head and ears, and was drowned in the melted butter.

Thumbikin

Piñoncito

A tale from Chile

Here is a charming thumbling tale from Chile. The Andean Mountain peaks play an important part in the mythology of Chile. Those snow-clad peaks loom over the country, beckoning with an air of mystery. So it is natural that the thumbling gets carried off to the mountains by a huge bird, perhaps a condor, though the story does not say. And he is restored to his true size by the bone of a giant found on the highest mountain peak.

*I*n a valley at the foot of the cordillera lived a man with his wife, good people who helped those who were poorer than themselves. They, themselves, were not wealthy. They lived by their own hard work. The man herded cattle and the woman made tamales, which she sold to passersby. Nevertheless the couple were sad, for they had no children.

One day an old man leaning on a cane passed through the valley. The woman was looking for grass for Blanquita, their little goat. When she saw the old man, she invited him into their home.

The old man was pleased to enter and sat himself down. He told the woman he was very tired as he had traveled far and had had nothing to eat but some pine nuts that he carried in his bag.

The good woman compassionately offered a plate of potatoes, and when the old man had finished those, she brought out hot tortillas from the oven. The old man thanked her and searched his bag to see if he had a coin for her, but no, there was nothing there but a single piñon nut. This he gave to her.

"I ask that God bless you for your kindness. This nut will be the father of your child."

The woman laughed heartily at these strange words and told her husband what the old man had said. A short time later the woman realized that she was going to have a baby! And after nine months she bore a little son. But he was *so* little, he was about the size of a pine nut. So he was called Piñoncito.

His parents were worried because Piñoncito did not grow. But they loved him enormously because he was very intelligent. When his father went up into the mountains and his mother went to do her marketing, Piñoncito stayed at home and placed himself in front of the door to guard the property.

However, one day when his mother went out to look for wood for the oven, warning her little son not to leave the house, Piñoncito disobeyed and ran off to play. He was trying to climb a stone, which to him seemed a rocky peak, when it began to rain heavily. In order not to get wet Piñoncito took shelter under a callampa plant.

It rained for a long time and the poor child didn't dare leave his refuge for fear of drowning. Just then a group of muleteers passed by with their mule train. One of these men picked the callampa plant and put it under his poncho, thinking he would eat it later. And quick as that, in went Piñoncito, and without saying a word.

When night came, the muleteers settled down under a huge rock that formed a cave and started a fire to warm themselves and cook a piece of meat they had brought with them. The one who had picked the callampa wanted to roast it. So he held the callampa plant over the flames.

"Ay! I'm burning! I'm burning!" cried a tiny voice.

It was Piñoncito who cried out.

"Caracole!" said one of the muleteers.

"Are fleas talking now?"

"Ay! I'm burning!" again screeched Piñoncito.

Then the man, a bit put out, threw into a corner the cigar he had been smoking and without further ado pulled the callampa from the fire and began to eat it.

Piñoncito gave him a bite on the lip! And the man, not knowing what sort of insect had stung him, threw the callampa away. It happened to fall near the mules, and as they were hungry, one of them ate up the callampa, swallowing at the same time Piñoncito. Thus it was that he found himself in the stomach of a mule.

At dawn the mule drivers took up again their travel with the animals. Piñoncito did not feel exactly happy in his little prison, because he could scarcely breathe. He asked himself how he was going to get out of this, but everything took care of itself shortly, for the mule felt he had butterflies in his insides while Piñoncito jumped about in them. So the mule soon solved the matter by relieving himself. With this the little boy fell out into the fresh air once more, totally dirty and smelling something awful, but happy to be in the world once more.

But here came a huge bird hunting twigs for its nest. It grabbed poor Piñoncito and carried him off to its mountaintop, to a rocky ledge where it kept its nest.

As soon as the bird left, Piñoncito looked around for something to eat. Since he was so tiny, it took very little to satisfy him. He could eat grass, flowers, almost anything he found, even sweet roots.

The bird had hatched its chicks and in the nest, chirping incessantly, sat two newborn chicks. Piñoncito hid himself between them and when the mother brought something for them to eat, the boy also opened *his* mouth and took food. The birds kept on growing and Piñoncito, having food and shelter, just stayed in the nest. One day he spied a serpent climbing up the rock, planning to eat his half-brother chicks. They still hadn't learned to fly, and they began to chirp desperately when they saw the snake approaching.

Piñoncito felt terrible for the poor helpless chicks and thought: "Now their mother will weep when she finds her nest empty."

Then he remembered that he had stuck into his cloth a needle to use as a sword. He hid by the nest, and when the serpent stuck out its tongue to grab the chicks, he, with his needle, pierced it! In pain, the animal fell from the rock and rolled headlong into the canyon.

At that moment the chicks' mother arrived and saw all that Piñoncito had done. She gave him thanks in her birds' tongue, and the little boy told her of his adventures. Because he was half fairy, he could understand the speech of animals.

To repay him for saving her children, the mother bird picked little Piñoncito up by his clothing and flew with him back to his own home.

"Take this bone of a giant which I found in the highest peak of the mountains. You have only to rub your body with this bone and you will grow to the same size as other children."

Piñoncito took the bone, but it was so heavy he could hardly carry it. As soon as he was once more in his house, he passed the bone all over his body.

His mother had gone out and when she returned, she was amazed to see her son, now transformed into a tall, strong lad, as big as others his own age. After they had embraced, crying with happiness, he told of his adventures. These same adventures have passed from mouth to heart and have become famous throughout all the world.

Tom Thumb

A tale from England

The earliest print versions of the thumbling "Tom Thumb" set the tale in King Arthur's court. In this tale, Tom Thumb is born when the magician Merlin, who takes people literally at their word, grants a peasant's wish for a son, "even though it should be no bigger than his thumb." The fairy queen of the court, with her elfin entourage, attends his christening and dresses him, with the result that he is referred to as a "fairy boy." The presentation of Tom's tale in rhyme was popular in seventeenth- and eighteenth-century England, explaining in part why this version frequently lapses into rhyme.

*I*n the merry days of good King Arthur, there lived in one of the counties of England a ploughman and his wife. They were poor, but as the husband was a strong workman, and his partner an able assistant in all matters pertaining to the farmhouse, the dairy, and poultry, they managed to make a very good living, and would have been contented and happy, had Nature blessed them with any offspring. But although they had been married several years, no olive branch had yet appeared, and the worthy couple sadly lamented their hard lot.

There lived at this period, at the court of Arthur, a celebrated conjuror and magician, whose name was Merlin, the astonishment of the whole world, for he knew the past, present, and future, and nothing appeared impossible to him. Persons of all classes solicited his assistance and advice, and he was perfectly accessible to the humblest applicant. Aware of this, the ploughman, after a long consultation with his "better half," determined to consult him, and, for this purpose, travelled to the court, and, with tears in his eyes, beseeched Merlin that he might have a child, "even though it should be no bigger than his thumb."

Now Merlin had a strange knack of taking people exactly at their words, and without waiting for any more explicit declaration of the ploughman's wishes, at once granted his request. What was the poor countryman's astonishment to find, when he reached home, that his wife had given birth to a gentleman so diminutive, that it required a strong exercise of the vision to see him. His growth was equally wonderful, for—

> *In four minutes he grew so fast,*
> *That he became as tall*
> *As was the ploughman's thumb in length,*
> *And so she did him call.*

The christening of this little fellow was a matter of much ceremony, for the fairy queen, attended by all her company of elves, was present at the rite, and he formally received the name of Tom Thumb. Her majesty and attendants attired him with their choicest weeds, and his costume is worth a brief notice. His hat was made of a beautiful oak leaf; his shirt was composed of a fine spider's web, and his hose and doublet of thistle-down. His stockings were made with the rind of a delicate green apple, and the garters were two of the finest little hairs one can imagine, plucked from his mother's eyebrows. Shoes made of the skin of a little mouse, "and tanned most curiously," completed his fairy-like accoutrement.

It may easily be imagined that Tom was an object of astonishment and ridicule amongst the other children of the village, but they soon discovered that, notwithstanding his diminutive size, he was more than a match for them. It was a matter of very little consequence to Tom whether he lost or won, for if he found his stock of counters or cherrystones run low, he soon crept into the pockets of his companions, and replenished his store. It happened, on one occasion, that he was detected, and the aggrieved party punished Tom by shutting him up in a pin-box. The fairy boy was sadly annoyed at his imprisonment, but the next day he amply revenged himself; for hanging a row of glasses on a sunbeam, his companions thought they would follow his example, and, not possessing Tom's fairy gifts, broke the glasses, and were severely whipped, whilst the little imp was overjoyed at their misfortune, standing by, and laughing till the tears run down his face.

The boys were so irritated with the trick that had been played upon them, that Tom's mother was afraid to trust him any longer in their company. She accordingly kept him at home, and made him assist her in any light work suitable for so small a child. One day, while she was making a batter-pudding, Tom stood on the edge of the bowl, with a lighted candle in his hand, so that she might see it was properly made. Unfortunately, however, when her back was turned, Tom accidentally fell in the bowl, and his mother not missing him, stirred him up in the pudding "instead of minced fat," and put the pudding in the kettle with Tom in it. The poor woman paid dearly for her mistake, for Tom had no sooner felt the warm water, than he danced about like mad, and the pudding jumped about till she was nearly frightened out of her wits, and was glad to give it to a tinker who happened to be passing that way. He was thankful for a present so acceptable, and anticipated the pleasure of eating a better dinner than he had enjoyed for many a long day. But his joy was of short duration, for as he was getting over a stile, he happened to sneeze very hard, and Tom, who had hitherto remained silent, cried out, "Hollo, Pickens!" which so terrified the tinker, that he threw the pudding into the field, and scampered away as fast as ever he could go. The pudding tumbled to pieces with the fall, and Tom, creeping out, went home to his mother, who had been in great affliction on account of his absence.

A few days after this adventure, Tom accompanied his mother when she went into the fields to milk the cows, and for fear he should be blown away by the wind, she tied him to a thistle with a small piece of thread. While in this position, a cow came by, and swallowed him up:

> But, being missed, his mother went,
> Calling him everywhere:
> Where art thou, Tom? where art thou, Tom?
> Quoth he, Here, mother, here!
> Within the red cow's stomach, here
> Your son is swallowed up;
> All which within her fearful heart
> Much woful dolour put.

The cow, however, was soon tired of her subject, for Tom kicked and scratched till the poor animal was nearly mad, and at length tumbled him out of her mouth, when he was caught by his mother, and carried safely home.

A succession of untoward accidents followed. One day, Tom's father took him to the fields a-ploughing, and gave him "a whip made of a barley straw" to drive the oxen with, but the dwarf was soon lost in a furrow. While he was there, a great raven came and carried him an immense distance to the top of a giant's castle. The giant soon swallowed him up, but he made such a disturbance when he got inside, that the monster was soon glad to get rid of him, and threw the mischievous little imp full three miles into the sea. But he was not drowned, for he had scarcely reached the water before he was swallowed by a huge fish, which was shortly after captured, and sent to King Arthur by the fisherman for a new-year's gift. Tom was now discovered, and at once adopted by the king as his dwarf;

> Long time he liv'd in jollity,
> Belov'd of the court,
> And none like Tom was so esteem'd
> Amongst the better sort.

The queen was delighted with the little dwarf, and made him dance a galliard on her left hand. His performance was so satisfactory, that King Arthur gave him a ring which he wore about his middle like a girdle; and he literally "crept up the royal sleeve," requesting leave to visit his parents, and take them as much money as he could carry:

Tom Thumb

And so away goes lusty Tom
With threepence at his back,
A heavy burthen, which did make
His very bones to crack.

Tom remained three days with the old couple, and feasted upon a hazel-nut so extravagantly that he grew ill. His indisposition was not of long continuance, and Arthur was so anxious for the return of his dwarf, that his mother took a birding-trunk, and blew him to the court. He was received by the king with every demonstration of affection and delight, and tournaments were immediately proclaimed:

Thus he at tilt and tournament
Was entertained so,
That all the rest of Arthur's knights
Did him much pleasure show.

And good Sir Launcelot du Lake,
Sir Tristram and Sir Guy,
Yet none compar'd to brave Tom Thumb
In acts of chivalry.

Tom, however, paid dearly for his victories, for the exertions he made upon this celebrated occasion threw him into an illness which ultimately occasioned his death. But the hero was carried away by his godmother, the fairy queen, into the land of Faerie, and after the lapse of two centuries, he was suffered to return to earth, and again amuse men by his comical adventures. On one occasion, after his return from fairy-land, he jumped down a miller's throat, and played all manner of pranks on the poor fellow, telling him of all his misdeeds, for millers in former days were the greatest rogues, as everybody knows, that ever lived. A short time afterwards, Tom a second time is swallowed by a fish, which is caught, and set for sale at the town of Rye, where a steward haggles for it,—

Amongst the rest the steward came,
Who would the salmon buy,
And other fish that he did name,
But he would not comply.

The steward said, You are so stout,
If so, I'll not buy any.

So then bespoke Tom Thumb aloud,
"Sir, give the other penny!"

At this they began to stare,
To hear this sudden joke:
Nay, some were frighted to the heart,
And thought the dead fish spoke.

So the steward made no more ado,
But bid a penny more;
Because, he said, I never heard
A fish to speak before.

The remainder of the history, which details Tom's adventures with the queen, his coach drawn by six beautiful white mice, his escaping on the back of a butterfly, and his death in a spider's web, is undoubtedly a later addition to the original, and may therefore be omitted in this analysis. It is, in fact, a very poor imitation of the first part of the tale.

Petit Poucet

A tale from France

*T*his is a quite different thumbling tale, made popular by Charles Perrault and known in France as "Petit Poucet" (Little Thumb). In this tale the thumbling is not a miniature child but merely the smallest of seven brothers. He is seen as very small, but not as small as a thumb. He is *called* "Little Thumb," and in some versions he is no bigger than a thumb when he is born. By the time the story takes place he is a real little boy, but a very small one.

In this story "Petit Poucet," who is scorned by his brothers at the beginning, saves them all from an ogre and brings them safely home, usually with the ogre's treasure.

*O*nce upon a time there lived a woodcutter and his wife, who had seven children, all boys. The eldest was only ten years old, and the youngest was seven. People were astonished that the woodcutter had had so many children in so short a time, but the reason was that his wife delighted in children, and never had less than two at a time.

They were very poor, and their seven children were a great tax on them, for none of them was yet able to earn his own living. And they were troubled also because the youngest was very delicate and could not speak a word. They mistook for stupidity what was in reality a mark of good sense.

This youngest boy was very little. At his birth he was scarcely bigger than a man's thumb, and he was called in consequence "Little Tom Thumb." The poor child was the scapegoat of the family, and got the blame for everything. All the same, he was the sharpest and shrewdest of the brothers, and if he spoke but little he listened much.

There came a very bad year, when the famine was so great that these poor people resolved to get rid of their family. One evening, after the children had gone to bed, the woodcutter was sitting in the chimney corner with his wife. His heart was heavy with sorrow as he said to her:

"It must be plain enough to you that we can no longer feed our children. I cannot see them die of hunger before my eyes, and I have made up my mind to take them tomorrow to the forest and lose them there. It will be easy enough to manage, for while they are amusing themselves by collecting fagots we have only to disappear without their seeing us."

"Ah!" cried the woodcutter's wife, "do you mean to say you are capable of letting your own children be lost?"

In vain did her husband remind her of their terrible poverty; she could not agree. She was poor, but she was their mother. In the end, however, reflecting what a grief it would be to see them die of hunger, she consented to the plan, and went weeping to bed.

Little Tom Thumb had heard all that was said. Having discovered, when in bed, that serious talk was going on, he had got up softly, and had slipped under his father's stool in order to listen without being seen. He went back to bed, but did not sleep a wink for the rest of the night, thinking over what he had better do. In the morning he rose very early and went to the edge of a brook. There he filled his pockets with little white pebbles and came quickly home again.

They all set out, and little Tom Thumb said not a word to his brothers of what he knew.

They went into a forest which was so dense that when only ten paces apart they could not see each other. The woodcutter set about his work, and the children began to collect twigs to make fagots. Presently the father and mother, seeing them busy at their task, edged gradually away, and then hurried off in haste along a little narrow footpath.

When the children found they were alone they began to cry and call out with all their might. Little Tom Thumb let them cry, being confident that they would get back home again. For on the way he had dropped the little white stones which he carried in his pocket all along the path.

"Don't be afraid, brothers," he said presently; "our parents have left us here, but I will take you home again. Just follow me."

They fell in behind him, and he led them straight to their house by the same path which they had taken to the forest. At first they dared not go in, but placed themselves against the door, where they could hear everything their father and mother were saying.

Now the woodcutter and his wife had no sooner reached home than the lord of the manor sent them a sum of ten crowns which had been owing from him for a long time, and of which they had given up hope. This put new life into them, for the poor creatures were dying of hunger.

The woodcutter sent his wife off to the butcher at once, and as it was such a long time since they had had anything to eat, she bought three times as much meat as a supper for two required.

When they found themselves once more at table, the woodcutter's wife began to lament.

"Alas! where are our poor children now?" she said; "they could make a good meal off what we have over. Mind you, William, it was you who wished to lose them: I declared over and over again that we should repent it. What are they doing now in that forest? Merciful heavens, perhaps the wolves have already eaten them! A monster you must be to lose your children in this way!"

At last the woodcutter lost patience, for she repeated more than 20 times that he would repent it, and that she had told him so. He threatened to beat her if she did not hold her tongue.

It was not that the woodcutter was less grieved than his wife, but she browbeat him, and he was of the same opinion as many other people, who like a woman to have the knack of saying the right thing, but not the trick of being always in the right.

"Alas!" cried the woodcutter's wife, bursting into tears, "where are now my children, my poor children?"

She said it once so loud that the children at the door heard it plainly. Together they all cried out:

"Here we are! Here we are!"

She rushed to open the door for them, and exclaimed, as she embraced them:

"How glad I am to see you again, dear children! You must be very tired and very hungry. And you, Peterkin, how muddy you are—come and let me wash you!"

This Peterkin was her eldest son. She loved him more than all the others because he was inclined to be redheaded, and she herself was rather red.

They sat down at the table and ate with an appetite which it did their parents good to see. They all talked at once, as they recounted the fears they had felt in the forest.

The good souls were delighted to have their children with them again, and the pleasure continued as long as the ten crowns lasted. But when the money was all spent they relapsed into their former sadness. They again resolved to lose the children, and to lead them much further away than they had done the first time, so as to do the job thoroughly. But though they were careful not to speak openly about it, their conversation did not escape little Tom Thumb, who made up his mind to get out of the situation as he had done on the former occasion.

But though he got up early to go and collect his little stones, he found the door of the house doubly locked, and he could not carry out his plan.

He could not think what to do until the woodcutter's wife gave them each a piece of bread for breakfast. Then it occurred to him to use the bread in place of the stones, by throwing crumbs along the path which they took, and he tucked it tight in his pocket.

Their parents led them into the thickest and darkest part of the forest, and as soon as they were there slipped away by a side path and left them. This did not much trouble little Tom Thumb, for he believed he could easily find the way back wherever he walked. But to his dismay he could not discover a single crumb. The birds had come along and eaten it all.

They were in sore trouble now, for with every step they strayed further, and became more and more entangled in the forest. Night came on and a terrific wind arose, which filled them with a dreadful alarm. On every side they seemed to hear nothing but the howling of wolves which were coming to eat them up. They dared not speak or move.

In addition it began to rain so heavily that they were soaked to the skin. At every step they tripped and fell on the wet ground, getting up again covered with mud, not knowing what to do with their hands.

Little Tom Thumb climbed to the top of a tree, in an endeavor to see something. Looking all about him he espied, far away on the other side of the forest, a little light like that of a candle. He got down from the tree, and was terribly disappointed to find that when he was on the ground he could see nothing at all.

After they had walked some distance in the direction of the light, however, he caught a glimpse of it again as they were nearing the edge of the forest. At last they reached the house where the light was burning, but not without much anxiety, for every time they had to go down into a hollow they lost sight of it.

They knocked at the door, and a good dame opened to them. She asked them what they wanted.

Little Tom Thumb explained that they were poor children who had lost their way in the forest, and begged her, for pity's sake, to give them a night's lodging.

Noticing what bonny children they all were, the woman began to cry.

"Alas, my poor little dears!" she said; "you do not know the place you have come to! Have you not heard that this is the house of an ogre who eats little children?"

"Alas, madam!" answered little Tom Thumb, trembling like all the rest of his brothers, "what shall we do? One thing is very certain: if you do not take us in, the wolves of the forest will devour us this very night, and that being so we should prefer to be eaten by your husband. Perhaps he may take pity on us, if you will plead for us."

The ogre's wife, thinking she might be able to hide them from her husband till the next morning, allowed them to come in, and put them to warm near a huge fire, where a whole sheep was cooking on the spit for the ogre's supper.

Just as they were beginning to get warm they heard two or three great bangs at the door. The ogre had returned. His wife hid them quickly under the bed and ran to open the door.

The first thing the ogre did was to ask whether supper was ready and the wine opened. Then without ado he sat down to table. Blood was still dripping from the sheep, but it seemed all the better to him for that. He sniffed to right and left, declaring that he could smell fresh flesh.

"Indeed!" said his wife. "It must be the calf which I have just dressed that you smell."

"*I smell fresh flesh*, I tell you," shouted the ogre, eyeing his wife askance; "and there is something going on here which I do not understand."

With these words he got up from the table and went straight to the bed.

"Aha!" said he; "so this is the way you deceive me, wicked woman that you are! I have a very great mind to eat you too! It's lucky for you that you are old and tough! I am expecting three ogre friends of mine to pay me a visit in the next few days, and here is a tasty dish which will just come in nicely for them!"

One after another he dragged the children out from under the bed.

The poor things threw themselves on their knees, imploring mercy; but they had to deal with the most cruel of all ogres. Far from pitying them, he was already devouring them with his eyes, and repeating to his wife that when cooked with a good sauce they would make most dainty morsels.

Off he went to get a large knife, which he sharpened, as he drew near the poor children, on a long stone in his left hand.

He had already seized one of them when his wife called out to him. "What do you want to do it now for?" she said; "will it not be time enough tomorrow?"

"Hold your tongue," replied the ogre; "they will be all the more tender."

"But you have such a lot of meat," rejoined his wife; "look, there are a calf, two sheep, and half a pig."

"You are right," said the ogre; "give them a good supper to fatten them up, and take them to bed."

The good woman was overjoyed and brought them a splendid supper; but the poor little wretches were so cowed with fright that they could not eat.

As for the ogre, he went back to his drinking, very pleased to have such good entertainment for his friends. He drank a dozen cups more than usual, and was obliged to go off to bed early, for the wine had gone somewhat to his head.

Now the ogre had seven daughters who as yet were only children. These little ogresses all had the most lovely complexions, for, like their father, they ate fresh meat. But they had little round gray eyes, crooked noses, and very large mouths, with long and exceedingly sharp teeth, set far apart. They were not so very wicked at present, but they showed great promise, for already they were in the habit of killing little children to suck their blood.

They had gone to bed early, and were all seven in a great bed, each with a crown of gold upon her head.

In the same room there was another bed, equally large. Into this the ogre's wife put the seven little boys, and then went to sleep herself beside her husband.

Little Tom Thumb was fearful lest the ogre should suddenly regret that he had not cut the throats of himself and his brothers the evening before. Having noticed that the ogre's daughters all had golden crowns upon their heads, he got up in the middle of the night and softly placed his own cap and those of his brothers on their heads. Before doing so, he carefully removed the crowns of gold, putting them on his own and his brothers' heads. In this way, if the ogre were to feel like slaughtering them that night he would mistake the girls for the boys, and vice versa.

Things fell out just as he had anticipated. The ogre, waking up at midnight, regretted that he had postponed till the morrow what he could have done overnight. Jumping briskly out of bed, he seized his knife, crying: "Now then, let's see how the little rascals are; we won't make the same mistake twice!"

He groped his way up to his daughters' room, and approached the bed in which were the seven little boys. All were sleeping, with the exception of little Tom Thumb, who was numb with fear when he felt the ogre's hand, as it touched the head of each brother in turn, reach his own.

"Upon my word," said the ogre, as he felt the golden crowns; "a nice job I was going to make of it! It is very evident that I drank a little too much last night!"

Forthwith he went to the bed where his daughters were, and here he felt the little boys' caps.

"Aha, here are the little scamps!" he cried; "now for a smart bit of work!"

With these words, and without a moment's hesitation, he cut the throats of his seven daughters, and well satisfied with his work went back to bed beside his wife.

No sooner did little Tom Thumb hear him snoring than he woke up his brothers, bidding them dress quickly and follow him. They crept quietly down to the garden, and jumped from the wall. All through the night they ran in haste and terror, without the least idea of where they were going.

When the ogre woke up he said to his wife:

"Go upstairs and dress those little rascals who were here last night."

The ogre's wife was astonished at her husband's kindness, never doubting that he meant her to go and put on their clothes. She went upstairs, and was horrified to discover her seven daughters bathed in blood, with their throats cut.

She fell at once into a swoon, which is the way of most women in similar circumstances.

The ogre, thinking his wife was very long in carrying out his orders, went up to help her, and was no less astounded than his wife at the terrible spectacle which confronted him.

"What's this I have done?" he exclaimed. "I will be revenged on the wretches, and quickly, too!"

He threw a jugful of water over his wife's face, and having brought her round ordered her to fetch his seven-league boots, so that he might overtake the children.

He set off over the countryside, and strode far and wide until he came to the road along which the poor children were traveling. They were not more than a few yards from their home when they saw the ogre striding from hilltop to hilltop, and stepping over rivers as though they were merely tiny streams.

Little Tom Thumb espied near at hand a cave in some rocks. In this he hid his brothers, and himself followed them in, while continuing to keep a watchful eye upon the movements of the ogre.

Now the ogre was feeling very tired after so much fruitless marching (for seven-league boots are very fatiguing to their wearer), and felt like taking a little rest. As it happened, he went and sat down on the very rock beneath which the little boys were hiding. Overcome with weariness, he had not sat there long before he fell asleep and began to snore so terribly that the poor children were as frightened as when he had held his great knife to their throats.

Little Tom Thumb was not so alarmed. He told his brothers to flee at once to their home while the ogre was still sleeping soundly, and not to worry about him. They took his advice and ran quickly home.

Little Tom Thumb now approached the ogre and gently pulled off his boots, which he at once donned himself. The boots were very heavy and very large, but being enchanted boots they had the faculty of growing larger or smaller according to the leg they had to suit. Consequently they always fitted as though they had been made for the wearer.

He went straight to the ogre's house, where he found the ogre's wife weeping over her murdered daughters.

"Your husband," said little Tom Thumb, "is in great danger, for he has been captured by a gang of thieves, and the latter have sworn to kill him if he does not hand over all his gold and silver. Just as they had the dagger at his throat, he caught sight of me and begged me to come to you and thus rescue him from his terrible plight. You are to give me everything of value which he possesses, without keeping back a thing, otherwise he will be slain without mercy. As the matter is urgent he wished me to wear his seven-league boots, to save time, and also to prove to you that I am no impostor."

The ogre's wife, in great alarm, gave him immediately all that she had, for although this was an ogre who devoured little children, he was by no means a bad husband.

Little Tom Thumb, laden with all the ogre's wealth, forthwith repaired to his father's house, where he was received with great joy.

Many people do not agree about this last adventure, and pretend that little Tom Thumb never committed this theft from the ogre, and only took the seven-league boots, about which he had no compunction, since they were only used by the ogre for catching little children. These folks assert that they are in a position to know, having been guests at the woodcutter's cottage. They further say that when little Tom Thumb had put on the ogre's boots, he went off to the Court, where he knew there was great anxiety concerning the result of a battle which was being fought by an army two hundred leagues away.

They say that he went to the king and undertook, if desired, to bring news of the army before the day was out; and that the king promised him a large sum of money if he could carry out his project.

Little Tom Thumb brought news that very night, and this first errand having brought him into notice, he made as much money as he wished. For not only did the king pay him handsomely to carry orders to the army, but many ladies at the court gave him anything he asked to get them news of their lovers, and this was his greatest source of income. He was occasionally entrusted by wives with letters to their husbands, but they paid him so badly, and this branch of the business brought him in so little, that he did not even bother to reckon what he made from it.

After acting as courier for some time, and amassing great wealth thereby, little Tom Thumb returned to his father's house, and was there greeted with the greatest joy imaginable. He made all his family comfortable, buying newly created positions for his father and brothers. In this way he set them all up, not forgetting at the same time to look well after himself.

Fereyel and Debbo Engal the Witch

A tale from Africa

*T*he source of this tale does not indicate which ethnic group told this story. But one thing is certain: The thumbling is once again put in the position of rescuing his siblings from an evil character.

In this delightfully scary variation of "Petit Poucet" the thumbling, Fereyel, repeatedly matches wits with the evil witch Debbo Engal. Especially effective is the scene in which the witch sharpens her knife. But this tale is unusual in its ending in which the brothers all ride witch Debbo Engal (who has changed into a donkey) until Fereyel tricks her into revealing herself.

A long time ago there lived a witch called Debbo Engal. She had ten daughters, who were beautiful girls whom all men sought after, and from time to time youths would make the long journey to the house where they lived, hidden away in the bush. But none of these young men ever returned to their villages again, although nobody knew the reason why.

Debbo Engal knew however. When young men called to see her lovely daughters she would pretend to be delighted to meet them, giving them palm wine to drink and serving them choice food until night fell. Then she would say:

"It is too late and the night is too dark for you to walk back to your homes through the bush. Why not stay the night here and then go home at daybreak in safety?"

The young men would gladly agree, and Debbo Engal would tell them to lie down around the fire she kept burning in the biggest hut in the compound, and soon all would be asleep.

The wicked witch would then sharpen her large knife, creep up to the lads and kill them silently one by one with the skill of long practice. Then in the morning she would eat them! Debbo Engal did not feed on rice or corn or yams. Only human flesh satisfied her cruel appetite.

Now in a village some miles away lived a woman who had ten sons, and they heard of the beauty of Debbo Engal's daughters and wanted to visit them. Their mother entreated the boys not to go.

"It is an evil compound. Keep away, my sons," she begged. "So many young men have gone, never to return, and I do not want to lose all my sons at once."

But the lads laughed at her fears and assured her that they could look after each other and that ten men would be a match for any woman. Besides, the daughters were said to be so very beautiful that none of the young men could rest until they had seen the maidens.

Early the next morning the ten brothers set off in high spirits, singing and laughing as they walked along the narrow paths which led through the bush to Debbo Engal's compound.

No sooner had they left their mother, than she gave birth to an eleventh son. But what a strange-looking child he was, being scarcely the size of his mother's little finger. Then he stood upright straight away, and spoke to her.

"Good mother," he said, his bright little black eyes gazing fixedly at her face, "where are my brothers?"

"They have gone to Debbo Engal's compound," she replied in amazement, wondering how it was that he knew he had any brothers.

At this, the little boy gave a shout, exclaiming:

"Then I must go after them to save them," and he ran swiftly down the path which his brothers had taken.

Very soon he saw the ten lads in the distance and called after them:

"Hey! Hey! Wait for me."

The brothers stopped and turned to see who was calling and when the tiny boy ran up to them, they stared open-mouthed. Presently one of them managed to say:

"Who are you, and what do you want?"

"My name is Fereyel, and I am your youngest brother," he replied.

"Indeed you are not, for there are only ten of us," they replied. "Now go away and leave us in peace."

"I want to come with you to save you from harm," said Fereyel.

At this the brothers were angry and began to beat him, saying:

"Don't be so silly! How can you be our brother? Now go away and leave us in peace."

They beat him so hard that he lay senseless on the ground, and then the unkind brothers went on their way towards Debbo Engal's home.

Some time later one of the brothers found a piece of beautiful cloth lying across the path.

"Look what I've found!" he exclaimed. "Some careless person has dropped this fine cloth. This really is a lucky journey, isn't it?"

He picked up the cloth, slung it over his shoulder, and continued on his way. But somehow the cloth seemed to get heavier and heavier and presently he said to the second brother:

"Will you carry this for me? It is so very heavy on my shoulder."

The second brother laughed at him for a weakling, but very soon he too found the cloth too heavy and passed it on to the third, and so it went on until it reached the eldest of the ten brothers. When he complained about the weight, a shrill voice from inside the cloth called out:

"I'm inside! That's why you find the cloth so heavy. It is Fereyel, your youngest brother."

The young men were furious, and shaking Fereyel out of the cloth, they beat him again and again until once more they left him lying senseless beside the path.

"That's the end of him," they said. "Lying little scoundrel."

So they went on their way, for it was a long journey, and they began to hurry since they had wasted some time in beating Fereyel. Suddenly one of the brothers kicked his toe against a piece of metal, and as he bent to pick it up he saw that it was a silver ring.

"What luck!" he exclaimed. "Somebody has dropped a ring and now it is mine," and placing it on his finger he swaggered happily along.

But after a few minutes his hand hung heavily at his side and it was all he could do to walk, so weighty had the ring become. Then the same thing happened with the ring as with the cloth, each brother taking turns to wear it but passing it on when it got too heavy until at last it reached the eldest.

"There's something odd about this ring," he said, and was just taking it off his finger when Fereyel's voice piped up saying:

"I'm inside! That's why it's so heavy," and he jumped out of the ring on to the ground.

The brothers were about to beat him again when the eldest said:

"He seems determined to follow us and he's certainly been very cunning about it. Leave him alone and let him follow us to Debbo Engal's place after all."

So on they went, until at last they reached the compound they were seeking and Debbo Engal came out to greet them.

"Welcome," she cried, "welcome to our home! Come and meet my daughters."

The ten girls were very lovely and the brothers could scarcely take their eyes away from them. They were led away to the largest hut and Debbo Engal brought them delicious food and drink. At first she did not see Fereyel, for he was hidden behind the eldest brother's foot, but suddenly she caught sight of him, picked him up and exclaimed:

"What a charming little fellow you are! Come with me to my hut, and I will see that you are properly looked after. Never have I seen anyone so tiny! You must stay with me and be mine."

The brothers were surprised when Fereyel allowed himself to be led away without protest, but they soon forgot all about him as they feasted and drank and danced with the ten beautiful girls.

Night came and the brothers talked about going home, but Debbo Engal persuaded them to stay where they were.

"There is no moon," she said, "and you might lose your way. There are many snakes and wild animals about at this season, too, so stay with us and return to your home by daylight tomorrow."

The lads needed little persuasion and soon began another dance, while Debbo Engal brought more palm wine to refresh them. At last, however, the ten boys and girls had to admit that they were too tired to stay awake any longer, and Debbo Engal lent the brothers some mats and pillows on which to rest in the large hut where the girls were already almost asleep.

The wicked witch went back to her hut and gave Fereyel a comfortable mat to sleep on, and a specially soft pillow for his head.

"There you are!" she said. "Go to sleep now, and do not wake until the morning. I shall sleep on the mat beside you, my little man, so you will be quite safe."

So saying, she lay down and closed her eyes and soon the compound was wrapped in silence.

Presently Debbo Engal sat up and bent over Fereyel to see if he was asleep. He closed his eyes and kept perfectly still. She stood up and went to the corner where she kept her big knife, but just as she was taking hold of it, Fereyel called out:

"What are you doing?"

Hastily replacing the knife, Debbo Engal said sweetly:

"Aren't you asleep yet, little man? Let me smooth your pillow for you," and she tidied his bed, shook up the pillow and begged him to sleep in peace.

Once again she lay down beside him, and once again Fereyel pretended to sleep, so that after an hour the wicked witch got up for the second time and took out her knife, ready to sharpen it.

"What are you doing?" called Fereyel again; so making some excuse, Debbo Engal came back to her bed and told him to go to sleep again.

For a long time after that all was quiet, but Fereyel did not sleep. He waited until the steady breathing of the woman on the mat beside him told him that she was asleep, then silently he crept out of the hut, and made his way to where his brothers and the ten beautiful maidens were.

Gently and silently he changed all their clothes, putting the white gowns the boys wore over the girls, and covering his brothers in the blue robes of the women. Then he returned to Debbo Engal's hut, lay down again and waited.

Sure enough, Debbo Engal soon woke with a start, and for the third time she crept to the corner of her hut, seized her knife and began to sharpen it. Fereyel didn't interrupt her this time, and she slipped out of the door, holding the gleaming blade in her hand. Stealthily she entered the young people's hut, bent over the ten sleeping forms wrapped in white clothes and cut their throats with practiced skill.

"Ah ha! They'll make me a splendid meal tomorrow," she muttered to herself as she lay down contentedly and fell asleep again.

As soon as he was sure Debbo Engal would not wake, Fereyel hurried into the big hut and shook each of his brothers by their shoulders.

"Get up! Get up!" he whispered. "Debbo Engal meant to kill you all, and had I not changed over your clothes she would have done so. Look!" and he pointed to the ten girls who lay with their throats cut. "The old witch thinks it is you she has killed."

The brothers needed no second bidding but tumbled hastily out of the door and began their journey home through the bush, anxious to get as far away from Debbo Engal as possible, before she woke up again.

But it was no use. As soon as the witch woke and discovered that Fereyel was no longer by her side, she rushed into her daughters' hut and saw that she had killed them by mistake in the darkness. Uttering a fearful cry, she called up the wind, mounted on its back and flew towards the brothers, who were as yet scarcely half-way home.

Fereyel saw her coming.

"Look out!" he shouted to his brothers. "Here comes the old witch."

The brothers were panic-stricken but Fereyel knew what to do. Seizing a hen's egg from under a bush, he dashed it on to the ground between them and Debbo Engal. The egg immediately turned into a wide, deep river and the young men were able to continue on their way.

Debbo Engal was furious and turned about at once and made for home. But the brothers had not got rid of her so easily, for she came back with her magic calabash and began to empty out all the water from the swiftly-flowing river. Soon there was not a drop left and she was able to continue her journey once more.

Fereyel saw her coming and shouted:

"Look out! Here comes the old witch again," while he seized a large stone and flung it in her path. Immediately it changed into a high mountain and the brothers continued on their journey, certain that Debbo Engal could not get them now.

But the witch was not defeated yet. She went back to her home on another puff of wind and fetched her magic axe. Then she hacked and chopped and chopped and hacked, until at last the whole mountain disappeared and she was able to continue on her way.

But she was too late. Just then Fereyel saw her coming again and gave his brothers a warning shout.

"Look out!" he cried, as they saw their village ahead, and with one final effort they reached their house. Debbo Engal knew she could not touch them there, and went away defeated, muttering fearful curses under her breath.

But Debbo Engal did not let the matter rest there. She was determined to get hold of the young men and kill them, even as she had mistakenly killed her own daughters, so she lay in hiding and waited her chance.

Early next morning the village headman told the brothers to go into the bush and collect logs. Somewhat fearfully, they went, keeping close together and glancing over their shoulders from time to time in case the witch turned up again. They did not see her however, for the very good reason that she had heard the headman's instructions and had immediately turned herself into a log of wood.

As the lads collected the logs they stacked them beside the path.

"Come on," one of them called to Fereyel. "Don't be so lazy! Why are you standing still while we do all the work?"

"Because Debbo Engal had turned herself into a log, and I do not want to be the one who picks her up," he explained.

On hearing this, the brothers threw down the logs they were carrying and raced for home. Debbo Engal, who was furious that she had not yet been picked up, changed herself back into a witch and hid in the bush, still longing for revenge.

A few days later the brothers went off into the bush to collect wild plums. At first they only found trees with somewhat withered fruit, but suddenly they came upon a bush with bright green leaves and luscious, juicy plums hanging from its branches.

"Look at this! What luck!" exclaimed the eldest brother, reaching out his hand to pluck the fruit.

"Stop!" commanded Fereyel. "Don't you realize that it's a magic tree, and Debbo Engal is inside it? If you fill your calabashes with the fruit, she'll soon have you under her spell."

The brothers dropped their calabashes and ran home with haste, and once again Debbo Engal's plans were frustrated.

The next morning when the brothers came out of their compound, they saw a grey donkey grazing on the communal grass at the edge of the village. It seemed to belong to no one and the brothers thought it must have strayed from a nearby village.

"What luck," said the eldest. "Let's all have a donkey ride!"

One by one they climbed on to the donkey's back, until all ten of them were perched up there precariously. Then they turned to Fereyel standing beside them and called:

"Room for one more. Jump on!"

"There's no room at all," replied Fereyel. "Even I, small as I am, could not get on that donkey's back now."

Immediately the strangest thing happened. The donkey began to grow longer, and there was plenty of room for Fereyel.

"Ah ha!" he shouted. "You won't catch me climbing on the back of such an elongated donkey."

Then much to everyone's surprise, the donkey shrank back to its normal size.

Fereyel laughed. "You have all been tricked again," he said. "Donkeys don't usually understand what human beings are saying. But this one does, so it must be Debbo Engal again. Get off, if you value your lives!"

The brothers tumbled off the donkey's back and the animal went braying back to the bush, where it changed into Debbo Engal.

Now the witch was desperate. She had tried all her magic tricks save one, and she was determined to make this a success.

"If I can only catch Fereyel, I shall be sure of the others," she said to herself, and sat in deep contemplation planning another wicked scheme.

The next morning a beautiful maiden walked into the village. The villagers crowded around her and asked why she had come.

"I want to see Fereyel," she replied in a clear bell-like voice. "Will you lead me to his house?"

Fereyel was amazed to see such an attractive girl, and asked her to come into the visitors' hut. Then he went out and killed a young goat and told his mother to cook the meat for his beautiful guest.

All day long he entertained the maiden, giving her delicious food to eat and talking to her all the while. The villagers, who had never seen such beauty before, came peeping into the hut from time to time and went away exclaiming loudly at the wonderful sight.

When evening came the maiden said she must go back to her home.

"Will you lead me through the bush, Fereyel?" she asked. "It is too dark for me to go alone."

Fereyel willingly agreed and the whole village turned out to bid them good-bye. It was very dark and Fereyel led the way along the little winding path that the maiden had told him led to her home. Suddenly she disappeared behind a thick tree-trunk, and was completely hidden. Fereyel stood still, alert and waiting, straining his eyes in the dark.

Then out slithered a horrible, fat python which made straight for Fereyel and would have coiled itself round him and crushed him to death had he not been waiting for this moment.

"Aha! Debbo Engal," he laughed, and changed himself into a roaring fire. The python had no time to turn round. It could not stop its huge, rippling body from dashing straight into the fire, where it immediately perished.

Great was the joy in Fereyel's village when he went home and told his brothers the tale, and great was the feasting and dancing they had that night to celebrate the death of the wicked witch, Debbo Engal.

Digit the Midget

An Amhara tale from Ethiopia

This thumbling tale at first appears similar to "Petit Poucet." A thumbling is mistreated by his seven older and bigger brothers. However, this is a quite different story. Here the thumbling doesn't *rescue* his brothers, but instead fuels the sibling rivalry by outwitting them at every turn, garnering his mother's favor at their expense. This is actually a trickster tale, with the thumbling cast as the main character. In this Ethiopian story, some ethnic flavor is introduced with the use of such words as "injera" (bread) and "wot" (stew).

A woman of Munz had seven large, strong, stupid sons. These sons went about the house breaking chairs with their weight, emptying the *injera* basket and the *wot* pot with their great appetites, and filling the house with the terrifying rumble of their snoring. Although they were very strong they never worked when they could avoid it. They ate, slept, snored, and got in the way of their poor, hard-working mother.

One day the poor woman of Munz could stand her house and family no longer. She ran away toward the Monastery of Saint Stephen on an island in Lake Haik. The woman was not allowed to go out to the island and the monastery. No woman had been allowed there since the monastery had been built hundreds of years ago. The woman from Munz knelt down on the lake shore, cast her eyes toward the holy monastery on the island, and cried in a loud voice, "Oh, God and all Your Angels and Saints, hear my prayer. I have been sent seven of the biggest, clumsiest, hungriest, and laziest sons in Ethiopia. Soon I am to have another child. I would like a daughter. But if You do not wish to send me the daughter, send me a small son."

Now God, Who hears all prayers but only answers some, did not send a daughter, but He did send a very small son. When Digit was born he was only half the length of a man's thumb. The woman of Munz was delighted with her little child. It was the first baby she had ever been able to carry in her arms. For all the other babies, the mother had had to hire a mule to bring them home.

When the days passed and Digit did not grow larger, the mother was even more pleased. And it was clear to her that Digit was a very clever baby and, later, a clever little boy. Digit had to be clever to dodge the feet of his huge, clumsy brothers. Often Digit's mother barely saved him from being crushed by one of his brother's elbows. Another time, when the door was left open, Digit was blown out into the yard by the breeze of his brothers' snoring. Digit's mother always kept him close to her, safe from mice and chickens.

As the years passed, the seven huge brothers came to hate Digit. Even when they had been babies and sick, their mother had never taken them on her lap. Their mother had never kissed them on the top of their heads. She had never even seen the tops of their heads. She had never hugged them because her arms would not fit around them. And once when the oldest brother hugged his mother he broke three of her ribs. It was clear that Digit was her favorite. She took the choicest meat from the *wot* for Digit, and the brothers had to crack the bones and pick out the marrow for him.

The brothers plotted and schemed to get rid of Digit. Once they persuaded him to steal the prize bull of their most terrible neighbor. The brothers thought that the terrible neighbor, who was a *cherak*, or man-eating monster, would catch and eat Digit. But Digit climbed into the bull's ear. When Digit wished the bull to turn right, Digit buzzed like a horse fly in the bull's left ear. The bull then turned right to escape the fly. To make a left turn, Digit walked all the way across the bull's neck and buzzed in the right ear. Digit took the bull right out from under the cherak's nose and guided it to the forest where the brothers waited.

The brothers were sorry that Digit escaped, but they were happy to get the bull. They made a big fire and killed and dressed the bull. The brothers then took all the choice meat for themselves and left Digit almost none.

Digit said, "Brothers, you are big men and you need the food. All I wish for is the bladder."

The brothers threw the bladder to Digit. Digit then puffed air into the bladder and made a drum. He began to beat on the drum with a stick and shout, "We stole your prize bull, Cherak. Come and get us if you dare. My big brothers aren't afraid of your evil spells."

The brothers were so frightened that they threw the meat on the ground and ran away into the forest. Digit went back to the cherak's house, stole a mule, and loaded the meat onto it. Digit brought the mule and the meat home and gave them to his mother. The mother made a stew of the hoofs and tail for the brothers.

Things grew worse between Digit and his brothers. The brothers complained, "Mama never hugs and kisses us. Does she ever call us little stalks of sugar? Never. With the little fiend gone, Mama would love us again."

Finally things became so bad that Digit had to move out of the house to his own little house. The mother was so angry that she made the brothers leave their home and get married.

One night the brothers came and burned Digit's house. But Digit was not killed. He slipped through a hole in the floor into the tunnel of a rabbit. Digit walked through the tunnel to safety.

The next morning Digit loaded the ashes of his house into sacks and had the sacks loaded onto mules. Digit decided to leave Munz to escape his brothers. On the road the first night Digit stopped at the house of a rich man. In the morning when Digit looked into his sacks, he began to scream, "Robbery! Thief! Some thief took my flour and filled the sacks with ashes."

Digit screamed and screamed, and the rich man felt very sorry for the poor little boy. The rich man did not want his neighbors to think that he would steal flour from a midget. So he gave Digit seven sacks of new flour. Digit decided to return home to give the flour to his mother.

When Digit returned home with the flour he told his brothers how he had tricked the rich man. "A very clever trick," all the brothers agreed. They went back to their own houses, burned them down and loaded the ashes onto the mules.

The first brother went to the home of the rich man and spent the night. The next morning he opened his sacks of ashes and began to scream that he had been robbed—just as Digit had done. But the rich man ordered him out of the house. When the second brother came along the next day and tried the same trick, the rich man had his servants throw him into the road. When the third brother came, the rich man ordered his servant to beat him with sticks.

When the fourth brother came to the house, the rich man asked, "What do you have in those sacks?"

"Flour," the stupid brother said.

"That is good. We are short of flour. We'll make your bread tonight from that flour."

That night the brother had to eat ashes bread, and the next day he was driven from the house. The rich man played the same trick on the fifth and sixth brother. But when the seventh brother came by, the rich man was tired of his joke. He turned the dogs loose on the seventh brother.

The brothers gathered around the bed of the seventh brother. "Digit must die," they decided.

One night while their mother and their wives slept, the brothers took Digit, pushed him into an *injera* basket and carried him to the river. The brothers tied down the lid of the basket and threw it into the river. They were certain that they would never see Digit the Midget again.

But the current of the river carried the basket along and washed it up on the shore. In the morning an Arab merchant named Yusef found the basket and opened it. Out hopped Digit. He began to dance and sing, "Oh, you are lucky. You are Allah's favored son."

"Why am I lucky?" the Arab asked. "I have only found a wet little boy on a river bank. What is lucky about that?"

Digit said, "Do I look unusual or strange?"

"You are unusually small," Yusef said.

"Yes. I am very small. For this reason I am the messenger of Allah. But for my small size I could not have fitted into this magic basket. And what a magic basket this is! Each day at noon it fills with gold."

Yusef was interested in a basket that filled with gold, but he was also greedy and worried. He said, "If I took that basket back to the town, the governor would take it from me."

"That is true," Digit agreed. "That is why Allah sent it to this wilderness."

"I have an idea," Yusef said. "I will stay here until the basket fills with gold many times. Then I will load the gold on mules. First I will hide the basket up in those rocks. I can give the governor some of my gold and come back for more whenever I need it."

"You are wise," Digit agreed. "It is a pleasure to find a man who is not so overcome with greed that he stops thinking. That plan sounds good. Where are your mules?"

The merchant struck himself on the forehead and began to pull at his beard. "What do I say! Fool, fool that I am. I sold my mules back at the last village and bought this fine horse to sell to the Sheik Mustafa."

"Very well," Digit said. "I will stay with the basket and the gold. You ride your fine horse to the village and bring back mules."

"Oh, no," said the greedy Yusef. "I will stay with the basket. You take this money and my horse and go for the mules. But you must tell no one about the magic basket."

"I will tell no one," Digit promised. "But do not worry. Only a very stupid man would believe such a story from a little boy."

Yusef laughed. "That is true," he agreed. "No one would believe such a story. Go, and be quick about it."

Digit took the money from the merchant, and climbed hand-over-hand up the horse's tail and onto the saddle. "I must tell you one other thing," Digit said. "You are new to the basket. If it does not bring gold on the noon of the first day, do not worry. You must be patient. The gold is worth waiting for."

"I will be patient," Yusef promised. "There will be thousands of noons to come. The first one does not matter."

Digit left Yusef sitting in front of the basket, and watching for the sun to reach the middle of the heavens. The horse was swift and strong, and Digit was at his home that night. Before giving the horse to his mother, Digit let all of his brothers see the horse and ride on it. But Digit would not tell them where he got the horse. He showed them the merchant's money and said that he had had many horses and sold them to get the money. Digit also gave the money to his mother.

"Why do you giant fools never bring me money or horses?" the mother screamed at her sons. "You bring me nothing but trouble. If it were not for the little one, we would all starve." The mother's words did not please her sons.

That night while the brothers filled the house with the rumble and thunder of their snoring, Digit crawled to the bed of his oldest brother. To his brother Digit whispered, "I found the horses in the river where you threw me. There are many more there. To-morrow while the others still sleep we will go there. When I whistle it will be the signal to rise and go to the river."

Digit then crept to the bed of his next oldest brother. "I found the horses in the forest. I tell only you of this. Tomorrow we will go there. I will whistle. Rise and follow me to the forest."

Digit told the next brother that the horses were on the mountain. To the next brother, Digit said that he had found the horses in the lake. He told the next brother that he found the horses on the desert, and the last brother was told to go to the meadow.

While the brothers were sleeping, and dreaming of horses, Digit tied all of their legs together.

In the morning Digit gave a shrill whistle through a hollow tube. The brothers rose and began to run in seven different directions. Enraged, because they were tied to-gether, they began to strike out and kick at one another. Finally they beat each other senseless.

Digit said to his mother, "I go after more horses."

"And where will you find them?" she asked.

"Wherever fools ride them," he told her.

Boy-Man

A Native American tale

*T*his tale features a small hero who acts much like thumblings the world over. He plays tricks on four large men and kills them one by one as they approach a door. He is swallowed by a fish and brings about its death. Despite these scrapes, however, the thumbling is a cocky and free spirit, ever confident in his ability to get out of trouble.

This tale, reprinted from a collection of Native American tales, is unique in that the only family member included is Boy-Man's sister, with whom he shares a close, loving bond. It is his sister who stands by, ready to help, as Boy-Man involves them in one adventure after another.

An enchanting scene in which fireflies play a part concludes this unusual tale.

*T*here was once a little boy who lived with his sister on the shore of a beautiful lake. This boy was not like other children,—he did not grow as they did, but remained as tiny a fellow as in his baby days.

The child's body, however, was no match for his spirit. He was a very giant in courage and he liked nothing better than to act the master of the lodge.

One winter day he said to his sister, "Make me a ball; I wish to go out on the ice and have some sport."

The girl did as she was asked, but as she gave it to him she warned him to take care of himself. "Don't go too far out on the ice," she begged.

Boy-man only laughed and started off in great glee, throwing his ball far ahead of him and running after it with the speed of the wind.

By and by he noticed some large spots on the ice ahead. When he drew nearer he found that these spots were four large men who were spearing fish. Strange to say, they looked so much alike that it was hard to tell one from another.

As Boy-man came close to them, one looked up and noticed the little fellow for the first time.

"Look!" he cried to the others, "see what a tiny creature that is."

His three brothers looked up at the same moment. They were so exactly alike that Boy-man said to himself, "Four in one; how hard it must be to choose their own hunting shirts!"

When they had done looking at Boy-man, the men turned once more to their fishing and paid no more attention to the little fellow.

"Hm!" thought he, not at all pleased. "They think because I am so tiny that I am not worth notice. I think I will teach them a little lesson."

The men had covered their heads in order to watch for the fish, so they did not see Boy-man as he crept close beside them and seized a large trout they had just caught. Then, holding it by its gills, he ran away over the ice. Feeling the jar from his footsteps, they looked up.

Boy-man was so small that at first they thought the fish was running away by itself. But when they got up, they could just see the little fellow's head above the fish he was carrying.

Boy-man ran home as fast as he could. He left the trout by the door and went inside, telling his sister to go out and bring in the fish. She was much surprised and cried out:

"Where did you get it? I hope you did not steal it."

Boy-man replied that it came from their lake and that he found it on the ice. Surely all the fish in its waters belonged to him.

"But *how* did you get it?" urged his sister.

"Never mind; get it ready for our dinner," was the reply.

Finding he would say nothing more, his sister did as she was bidden and the big fish was soon cooked. How sweet it tasted! It was no wonder the girl forgot everything else but the delicious dinner, and she asked her brother no more questions.

The very next morning he took his ball and started for the lake once more. He had great sport as he went. Sometimes he would hurl the ball far ahead of him; again, he would toss it high into the air above his head; and then he would throw it behind him and run back to get it, as though he did not care which way he went, so long as he was moving swiftly.

How fast he did run, to be sure! No one could have kept up with him, no matter how hard he might try.

Pretty soon Boy-man reached the lake. There were the four men fishing just as they had been the day before. "Now for more sport!" he thought. He took his ball and tossed it so far that it dropped into the hole in the ice around which the men were fishing. Then he called out:

"Please get my ball and give it to me."

"Indeed we will not," they answered with an ugly laugh. At the same time they took their spears and pushed the ball under the ice. When Boy-man saw what they had done, he cried out:

"Very well. Now look out!"

In a moment he had rushed upon the men and pushed every one of them into the water. At the same time the ball bounded out upon the ice. Boy-man picked it up and, tossing it ahead of him, ran gaily homeward. He moved so fast that he reached it ahead of the ball. There he stayed quietly and rested for the remainder of the day without saying anything about what had happened.

In the meantime the four men managed to get out of the water, but they were icy cold and wet and very angry.

"It is of no use to run after him," they said, "but we will yet punish him as he deserves."

Early the next morning they got ready to seek Boy-man in his own home. Their old mother begged them to think no more of revenge. She said:

"That little boy is certainly a manito, or he could not do such wonderful things."

Her sons did not listen to this good advice, but with such a terribly warcry as nearly frightened all of the birds of that neighborhood out of their feathers, they went in search of Boy-man.

When they were still a long way off he heard them coming, but he was not the least bit troubled. By and by his sister caught the sound of snow-shoes moving over the snow. She went to the door and there in the distance she saw the four big men coming toward the lodge. She was terribly frightened for her brother had told her he had made someone very angry the day before.

"Oh!" she cried, running to her brother. "That man is coming, but he has made himself into four."

"Never mind! Get me something to eat," was the cool answer.

"What! Can you eat now?" she asked in wonder.

His only answer was to tell her to do as he had asked her to and be quick.

She set the food before her brother and he began to eat. By this time the four brothers had reached the door. Just as they were about to lift the curtain, Boy-man turned his dish over. Instantly the doorway was blocked by a big stone.

The men outside, more angry than ever, began to pound and hammer with all their might. After a while they managed to make a small hole through the stone. Then one of the brothers, putting his face to the hole, rolled his eye round in a fearful way as though he expected to scare Boy-man by doing so.

But the little fellow went on with his meal in the coolest way, only stopping to send an arrow from his bow to the door. It entered the man's head and he fell back quite dead.

"Number one," remarked Boy-man quietly, and he paid no further heed to what he had done.

And now a second face appeared in the opening and a second arrow flew from Boy-man's bow. The head disappeared and the man fell as his brother had fallen. The tiny master of the lodge cried out, "Number two," and went on eating.

He treated the remaining two brothers in the same way. Then he told his sister to go outside and look about. As soon as she had done so, she hurried back, saying:

"Why, there are four of them!"

"Yes, and there will always be that number," he replied.

With these words, he himself went out and lifted the bodies from the ground. He gave a push to each, placing the first one with his face toward the East, the second toward the North, the third toward the West, and the fourth toward the South, and sent them flying in all directions.

The rest of the winter passed away quietly for Boy-man and his sister. But when spring came and the bright sun shone down upon the fresh green earth, the little fellow told his sister to make him some new arrows. She did as he told her, and fashioned them in the most careful way possible. She gave them to her brother, saying:

"Do not shoot into the lake, I pray you."

But Boy-man paid no heed to her words; he only turned toward the water and shot one of his arrows. Then he waded into the lake deeper and deeper. As his sister watched him, she cried out in great fright:

"Come back! O do come back!"

He did not answer her, but cried out:

"You of the red fins! Come and swallow me!"

Close beside Boy-man a great fish instantly appeared and swallowed him.

The poor sister standing on the shore was terribly frightened; but even as her brother was disappearing down the monster's throat he called out to her:

"Me-zush-ke-zin-ance!"

What could Boy-man mean by this? His sister did not understand.

"I wonder if it is an old moccasin that he wants?" she said to herself.

She hurried back to the lodge and got the moccasin. Tying it to a string fastened to a tree on the shore, she threw it into the water. The monster fish saw it.

"What is that?" he asked.

"It is a great dainty. Taste it," Boy-man answered.

The big fish did not question the strange command but hastened to obey. As soon as he had fairly swallowed it, Boy-man, who was laughing softly, seized the string and pulled himself ashore.

The sister was very much surprised to see the fish coming nearer and nearer, till at last he landed clear up on the beach. She was still more astonished when the monster seemed to speak, saying:

"Hurry up and let me out of this horrid place."

But no! It was the voice of her own brother. The girl was used to doing whatever he told her, so she at once took a knife and cut open the side of the fish. Out through this queer door stepped Boy-man.

"Cut up the fish and dry it," he ordered. "We shall have enough to eat for the whole spring."

"My brother is certainly wonderful," thought his sister after this thing had happened.

One evening they were sitting together in the lodge in the darkness when the girl said to her brother:

"It seems strange to me that you who have so much power cannot do more than Ko-ko, who gets all his light from the moon. It shines or not, as it pleases."

"Do you not think that is enough?" asked Boy-man.

"Yes," was the answer, "if it did not stay in the clouds, but would come into the lodge when we wish."

"You shall see that we have a light," declared her brother.

He stretched himself on a mat by the doorway and began to sing a chant to the fire-flies. They heard his voice and hastened to obey his call. First, one by one, then in great swarms, they came flying into the lodge till it was ablaze with their soft and beautiful light.

Boy-man and his sister looked at each other with trust and love in their faces. From that time they lived together in the little lodge in great happiness, and never did a doubt of the other enter the mind of either one.

The Snail *Choja*

A tale from Japan

This story is not really a thumbling tale. But it is so like many thumbling stories that I thought it interesting to include for comparison. The child here is a snail, but his early adventures are similar to those of many thumblings. In addition, he takes a bride. Unique to this tale is an especially moving episode in which the love of the bride for the thumbling is portrayed. It is her touching devotion to her husband that ultimately transforms the snail child into a handsome young man. This contains a spiritual aspect not seen in other thumbling tales.

*L*ong, long ago, there lived in a certain place a *choja* [rich man]. The people in the village said that he was so rich that he could not possibly be in need of anything.

Among the farmers who cultivated the rich man's estate, there were one man and his wife who were so poor that they sometimes had nothing at all to eat. They were already over forty years old, but for some reason or other they had no children. Every night before they went to bed, they would lament the fact that they were childless, saying to one another, "Oh, how much we would like to have a child; how nice it would be to have something to call our own child, even if it were only a frog or a snail." They often went to the shrine of the water deity and prayed that they might have a child.

One day, going out as usual to cut the grass growing along the edge of the rice fields, the farmer's wife prayed with all her heart to the water deity. "Honorable Water Deity, please give me a child, even if it is only like one of the snails here in the rice fields. I beg of you, hear my prayer."

As she said this, for some reason her stomach began to hurt. She tried her best to bear the pain, but it gradually became worse and worse, until finally she could no longer endure it and had to crawl home on her hands and knees. Her husband, greatly worried, tried to ease the pain, but no matter what he did, it did not get any better. There was no money with which to pay the doctor even if they were to call one; they were completely at a loss as to what to do. Fortunately a midwife lived in the neighborhood, and although she was not a doctor, they decided to call her. They did so and found that the farmer's wife was going to give birth to a baby. Upon hearing this, they were overjoyed and immediately lighted a candle before the *kamidana* [household shrine] and prayed that the water deity would help the baby to be born safely.

Shortly after this the wife gave birth to a tiny baby snail. Everyone was very much surprised, but since it was sent from the water deity, they determined to take very good care of it. They put it in a bowl of water and set it in front of the *kamidana*.

Twenty years passed. Strangely enough the Snail Boy grew no larger. He never spoke a word; however, he ate as much as anyone. One day, as the old farmer was loading the horses with the *nengumai* [yearly rice tax] which had to be paid each year to the *choja* who owned the land, he sighed to himself: "Ahh, ahh, it was generous of the water deity to give us a

child, and we are very thankful, but it is a snail child. Since he is only a snail, he cannot help me at all, and I have had to work all my life, taking care of my wife and this child."

Just as he was lamenting his fate, he heard a voice coming from somewhere: "Father, father, I'll deliver the rice for you." The old man looked around but saw no one. "This is strange," he thought. "Who could that be?"

"It is I, father. For a long time you have taken good care of me, and it is now time for me to go out into the world. Today I will take the rice to the master for you."

"But how will you drive the horses?"

"Since I am only a snail, I can't actually drive the horses, but if you put me up on one of the bales of rice, the horses can go along by themselves with no trouble at all, and I'll just ride along."

The old man was greatly surprised to hear that the Snail Boy, who until then had never spoken a word, could not only talk but even wanted to go and deliver the rice to the land-owner. However, since the Snail Boy had been sent by the water deity, the old man was afraid that he might be punished if he refused to do as requested. He loaded up the rice on the three horses, then took the Snail Boy from the bowl in front of the *kamidana* and put him up on top of one of the rice bales.

"Well, father and mother, I'll go and be back soon," said the Snail Boy, as he started off. "*Haido, haido shishi*" [get up, get up]; calling out to the horses like an expert driver, he drove out the gate and down the road.

The old man had let the boy take the horses, but he could not help worrying about whether everything would be all right; so he secretly followed along behind. However, the Snail Boy drove the horses like a real horseman; when he came to a ford or a bridge, he would call out, "*haai, hai, shan shan*" [whoa, easy now], in a loud voice, just like a real driver. And not only this, he sang the songs that drivers sing in a loud clear voice, so that the horses fell into step with the song, the bells on their necks going *janka, gonka,* jingle, jangle, in tune with the song, and so they went merrily on their way.

The people walking along the road and the people working in the rice fields heard a voice but saw no one driving the horses. They thought it very, very strange. "Those skinny horses certainly belong to that poor farmer, but who is singing the driver's songs?" they wondered, looking on in astonishment.

The boy's father, seeing everything that took place, wondered how it had all come about. He hurried back home and knelt down in front of the *kamidana* with his wife.

They prayed: "Oh, honorable Water Deity, hear our prayer. We have been so ignorant. You have given us such a wonderful son, and we have treated him so miserably. We beg you to protect him and guide him and the horses safely to the *choja*'s house."

The Snail Boy drove along without any trouble and came to the *choja*'s house. The servants, hearing that someone had come to deliver the yearly rice tax, went out to the front gate, but they saw only the horses; no one was with them. "What is this," they said; "the horses couldn't have come by themselves." But as they were talking they heard a voice from the midst of the rice bales, "I've brought the yearly rice tax; please let me down."

"What! Who's up there? We don't see anybody," they called out. They searched through the rice bales and found the tiny Snail Boy.

"I'm sorry to trouble you," the Snail Boy said, "but since I'm so small, I'm not able to unload the rice myself; won't you please do it for me? Be careful not to crush me. Just put me over there on the edge of the verandah, and I'll be quite safe."

The servants were very astonished to see the snail and hear it talking and immediately called the *choja*. "Master, master, a snail has come bringing the yearly rice tax."

The master of the house went out to see, and sure enough, there was the snail with the rice, just as the servants had said. Soon everyone in the whole house came out to see, exclaiming that this was the strangest thing they had ever seen.

Soon the rice was all unloaded as the snail had directed and was piled up in the storehouse; then the horses were given some hay. The Snail Boy was invited into the house for dinner. He perched up on the edge of the tray, and although no one could tell just how it happened, the rice in the bowl gradually became less and less. Next the soup began to diminish, and then the fish slowly disappeared.

At last the Snail Boy finished. He thanked his hosts for the delicious meal and asked if he might be served tea.

The *choja* had heard that the child which had been sent by the water deity to one of the farmers on his estate was a snail, but he did not know that the Snail Boy was able to talk and work just like a real person. The *choja* decided that in some way or other he would keep him as his own.

Thinking that he might be able to keep the Snail Boy without paying anything for him, the *choja* made a proposition, saying, "You know, Snail Boy, ever since your grandfather's time, your family and my family have had friendly relations with one another. Now, I have two daughters, and if you like, you may have one of them as your wife."

The Snail Boy, hearing this, was overjoyed and asked if it were really true.

"Quite true," said the *choja*. "I promise that I will give you one of my daughters as your wife."

So the Snail Boy, having been well entertained, returned home. His father and mother were beginning to get very worried, since it was becoming late and he had not come home; they feared that something had happened to him on the way. But just then he returned in high spirits; bringing the three horses with him.

During supper he told how he had been offered one of the *choja*'s daughters as his wife. His father and mother could hardly believe that it was true, but since the Snail Boy had been given to them by the water deity, they felt that it must be so. Just to make sure, they decided to ask the boy's aunt to go and see if the *choja* really meant what he had said.

When the aunt arrived at the *choja*'s house, he called his two daughters and said, "Which one of you would like to go to be the bride of the Snail Boy?"

The older sister cried out in disgust: "What! Get married to a filthy snail! It makes me sick to think of it!" She stamped her foot angrily and flounced out of the room.

The younger sister, however, was very gentle and kind. "Since you have promised that one of us should go to be the snail's bride, I will go. Please do not worry any more," she said reassuringly.

The aunt, hearing this answer from the *choja*, returned to the old man and his wife and told them all that had happened.

When it came time for the *choja*'s younger daughter to go to the Snail Boy's house for the wedding, the dowry was so large that not even seven horses could carry it. There were seven chests of drawers and seven trunks of kimonos; there were more pieces of hand baggage than one could count. Since they could not get it all into the poor farmer's house, the *choja* built a special storehouse to put it in. The bridegroom could furnish nothing, and since there were no relatives except the one aunt, the only guests at the wedding were the old father and mother, the aunt, and an old woman who lived close by.

The old man and his wife were very happy to have such a beautiful daughter-in-law. She was a great help to them, going out in the fields and working very hard all day, and so their lives became more comfortable and pleasant than they had ever known before. Feeling that all this had been given them by the water deity, they came to believe in him more and more devoutly.

After some time had passed, the day for the daughter-in-law to return to visit her parents drew near. It was decided that she should go soon after the festival which was always held on the eighth of April in honor of Yakushi-*sama* [Buddhist deity of healing], one of the patron deities of the village.

Spring came and the flowers began to bloom. Soon the eighth of April arrived and with it the festival of Yakushi-*sama*. The Snail Boy's bride decided that she would go and see the festival celebrations; so she carefully powdered her face, chose a beautiful kimono from one of the trunks, and put it on. She was so beautiful that she looked almost like a person from heaven. Having finished her dressing, she suggested to her snail husband, "Let's go together and enjoy the festival."

"Yes, let's do that," he agreed. "It's such nice weather today, and I haven't been out of doors for a long time." And so the beautiful bride put the snail in the fastener in the front of the sash of her kimono, and they set off together for the festival.

The girl walked along with the snail in her sash, the two of them talking and laughing together. The people they passed along the road shook their heads saying, "Ah, it's a pity, such a beautiful girl talking and laughing to herself; too bad that she has lost her mind."

The two of them went on until they came to the outer entrance of Yakushi-*sama's* shrine. Then the snail said to his wife: "I'm sorry, but for some reason, I can't go into the shrine with you. Just put me down here along the edge of the road by one of the rice paddy paths; you go by yourself and worship at the shrine. I'll wait for you here."

"Oh, really? Well, do be careful and don't let a bird or something eat you up. Wait just a moment, and I'll go up and say a prayer and be back very quickly." Saying this, she went up the hill to the main temple, where she prayed. She then hurried back to where she had left her husband, but he was not there. Greatly surprised, she searched hither and thither, but he was nowhere to be found.

Thinking that perhaps a bird might have eaten him up or that he might have fallen into the middle of the rice fields, she waded out into the rice paddies and searched everywhere. Since it was April, there were many, many snails in the muddy fields, and she picked them up one by one; but although they were all snails, none of them looked like her husband.

Snail, my snail,
Oh, my husband.
Ah, it is spring,
An evil old crow
Might have swooped down
And eaten you.

Singing this song, she searched in the muddy water until her face was splattered and her beautiful kimono was completely covered with mud. It began to grow late, and people returning from the festival saw the girl wading in the mud. "Such a beautiful girl," they said; "how sad it is that she has lost her mind."

No matter how much she searched, she was unable to find her husband. Giving up in despair, she decided to throw herself down where the mud was deepest and drown. Just as she was about to fling herself face down in the mud, she heard a voice behind her saying, "Here, here, girl! What are you doing?"

She looked around, and there stood a handsome young man. He had a straw hat on his head and at his waist hung a flute. The girl told the young man all that had happened, then said, "Now, I am going to drown myself."

"You needn't worry any more," the young man said; "I am the snail that you were looking for."

The girl, thinking that what he said was impossible, refused to believe him.

"You should not doubt me," he said; "I am the child sent by the water deity. Up until now I have been disguised as a snail, but today, since you went to worship at the shrine of Yakushi-*sama*, I could first appear in human form. I went to worship at the water deity's shrine, and when I came back here you were gone. I have been searching every-where for you."

Hearing this, the girl was filled with joy, and the two of them happily returned home together. While everyone had said that the girl was beautiful, the young man was no less handsome. When the young couple entered the house, the happiness of the young man's father and mother was beyond all description.

They immediately went to tell the *choja* what had happened. He came with his wife to see the snail son-in-law who had been changed into a real man. They were overjoyed upon seeing him, saying, "With such a handsome son, it is a shame that they should live in such a wretched hovel; let us build a mansion for them." So in the best part of the village they built a splendid big house, and the young man and his wife became merchants. The news that this was the young man who had been a snail was soon spread throughout the surrounding countryside, and his business prospered until it was not long before he was the richest man in the village.

The young man's aged father and mother were able to spend the rest of their lives in ease, and arrangements were made for the aunt to marry into a fine family. The young man became known as the Snail *Choja*, and he and all his relatives became very, very prosperous and wealthy.

The Diminutive Flute Player

A tale from Myanmar (Burma)

*I*n this tale gluttony almost results in the permanent downfall of this unambitious thumbling, who just sits around all day playing his flute and eating rice. Concerned that the thumbling's voracious appetite will wipe out the family's resources, his father contrives ways in which to get rid of the thumbling once and for all. But like a bad penny, the thumbling keeps coming back, none the worse for wear and even bearing gifts. Eventually both of his parents come to see that the thumbling is worth having around after all.

Once a poor woman gave birth to a son, who was no bigger than her thumb, and he fell through a hole in the flooring. "Where is my child? Where is my child?" the mother cried and looked everywhere. "Here I am," replied the child, climbing up a post and reappearing through the hole in the flooring. He had a flute in his hands and he played a melodious tune on it, which delighted the mother. "Mother, I have played you a tune," he said, "so please cook me a basket of rice." And when it was cooked, he gulped it down in no time.

Every day the diminutive flute player did nothing but play upon his flute and eat a basket of rice. The father, who was a poor cultivator, felt that he would soon be ruined by this glutton of a son. So he decided to kill the diminutive flute player, and asked the consent of his wife. But the woman loved her son dearly, and would not agree for a long time. In the end, as the man was so persistent in asking for her consent, she agreed. However, she stipulated that the killing should be done indirectly and as if accidentally and that, if the child should remain alive after four attempts, no further attempt should be made on the child's life.

The next day, the father asked his diminutive son to accompany him to the forest. When they arrived at the forest the father started to cut down a big tree and, just as the tree was about to fall, he asked his son to stand where the tree would fall. The child took his place, and the tree fell. The father thought that the boy had been killed and went home quickly. Soon after, the diminutive flute player arrived carrying the tree on his shoulder and shouting "Where shall I put the tree, father? I caught it on my shoulder and brought it here myself for firewood." So the first attempt to kill the flute player failed.

The next day the father took the son for a walk on the high road, and when a herd of elephants approached the father said to the flute player, "Stand in the middle of the road, and do not go away until I come back." The child obeyed and stood in the middle of the road, playing on his flute. The elephant-drivers could not see the flute player as he was small, but heard the flute. "Make way, make way," they shouted, looking up and down the road, but as they could not see anybody they drove the elephants forward. When the elephants were nearly on top of him the diminutive flute player jumped inside the hoof-mark of a cow, and the heavy feet of the elephants passed above his head harmlessly. The father came back, and was sorely disappointed to find his son alive and playing on his flute as usual.

The next morning the father asked the flute player to come fishing with him, and father and son went off in a boat. When the boat was some distance from the shore the father gave a push and the flute player fell into the water. The father rowed swiftly back to the shore thinking that his son was drowned, but he found the flute player waiting for him on a sandbank near the shore, astride a crocodile. "Father," greeted the son cheerfully, "I have caught a big water lizard for you." He stepped on to the boat, and the crocodile swam away. Thus, the father's third attempt to kill his son also ended in failure.

The next morning the father took the diminutive flute player to the thickest part of the forest, and slipped behind some trees. The flute player thought that his father had lost him, and wandered about the jungle crying "Father, I am here!" The father went home swiftly. At last the flute player decided to go home by himself. As he passed by a tiger's den the animal, smelling human flesh, rushed out but it stood stock still when it heard the flute player's music. The tiger was frightened of the little man who could make such a lot of loud noises. The flute player jumped onto the tiger's back and drove it towards his house, still playing on his flute. When he reached his home the child shouted cheerfully, "Father, I have brought a big cat for you." He jumped down and the tiger ran back to the forest. The mother took the diminutive flute player in her arms in great joy, and the father had to admit that he was a wonderful little fellow after all.

Three Inch

A tale from Pakistan

As in so many thumbling tales, the thumbling in this story, aptly named Three Inch, must overcome a series of obstacles in order to attain his goal, this time to marry a beautiful princess. After doing a good deed for a friendly frog, he receives a gift destined to make the princess his bride. But Three Inch must also free his father from slavery.

Although very serious in reaching his goals, Three Inch still has time to play the prankster, this time with a blacksmith even smaller than himself!

*T*here once was a poor woodcutter's wife who had no children. She and her husband prayed long to the goddess who gives children and at last the goddess appeared before the couple. She gave the wife a small cucumber. "Wait seven days," said the Goddess. "Then swallow this cucumber whole. You will have a child."

But the woodcutter's wife was so impatient that she ate the cucumber the very next day. What a tragedy! Instead of a baby, she gave birth to a tiny man, just three inches tall. He was fully grown at birth and could speak as well as any adult. But he was very ugly. And he had a long strand of black hair that hung down his back and trailed two feet behind him!

His parents were so embarrassed by his presence that his father went to the king and sold himself away as a slave. When Three Inch realized the suffering he had caused he vowed to make things right. He went straight to the king and begged him to free his father. The king was disgusted by this small, ugly creature but he said, "I will free your father if you bring me ten thousand rupees."

So Three Inch set off to try to accumulate that huge sum of money. As he was puzzling over the problem he looked up to see a huge black cloud right over his head. Three Inch started to run for shelter, thinking it was a rainstorm, but he felt a tug on his long hair and turned around. This had not been a rain cloud. The sky had been darkened for Three Inch by a huge frog leaping over his head. The frog laughed at Three Inch's surprise.

"I had heard that you were the woodcutter's son," croaked the Frog. "But a woodcutter's son should carry an axe. Where is your axe?"

Three Inch did not have an axe.

"Well, go down the road a bit and visit the blacksmith who lives there. He will sell you an axe for one rupee."

Three Inch didn't even have one rupee. But he went down the road anyway to find an axe. What a surprise he got when he saw the blacksmith. That blacksmith was even tinier than Three Inch. And he had a beard four feet long! The blacksmith was busy working and had not noticed Three Inch's arrival. Three Inch could not resist playing a joke on the tiny blacksmith. The end of the blacksmith's long beard was trailing into the bushes. Three Inch crept over and tied it tight to a log. Then he ran back and called "Hello, Blacksmith!" The little blacksmith stood up and started walking toward Three Inch, but his beard caught him up and he fell over onto his face. Three Inch thought that was a good joke. But the blacksmith was furious.

"Oh, don't be so grumpy," said Three Inch. "I'm still young and I like to play practical jokes. I will untie your beard if you will let me borrow your axe for a few days."

The blacksmith was in no position to argue. So he let Three Inch borrow the axe and Three Inch ran back to the Frog.

"Good. Now you have an axe and you are a proper woodcutter's son. See if you can use that axe. My wife is locked inside this oak tree. If you can chop it down, she will be freed."

Three Inch began to chop and chop at the oak tree. And after a while, sure enough, there sat the frog's wife, right in the middle of the tree. The frog was so happy that he gave Three Inch a present.

"Here is a small flask of green liquid. This is special liquid. Take it to the palace. The king has a beautiful daughter who has become blind. This liquid will cure the princess."

Three Inch thanked the frog, took the axe back to the little blacksmith, and hurried off to the palace.

"Your Majesty, I have come to marry your beautiful daughter!" announced the tiny man.

The King was amazed at the impertinence of this tiny creature. He turned his back on him, but he said, "When the eight thieves from beyond the twelve rivers are brought to me, then I will consider my daughter's wedding."

Three Inch started at once on the journey. That night he crossed the twelve rivers. And by daybreak he had reached the thieves' campfire. They were sitting around the fire counting the booty from their evening's work. Three Inch climbed onto an ant hill and addressed them.

"Gentlemen, I bring news from the king who lives across the twelve rivers. He is seeking a wealthy husband for his beautiful daughter. Since you possess so much gold, he would like to choose one of you as the bridegroom."

The thieves were surprised and delighted. They followed Three Inch right back to the king's palace.

"The King will see you one at a time," said Three Inch. "Come when I call you."

Then Three Inch climbed a low hanging tree beside the King's door and began to call the thieves. As each thief passed under the tree limb, Three Inch clopped it over the head and the thief fell forward into the King's throne room. The King's men were amazed to see the thieves fall one by one into the King's presence. They stacked the bodies in the corner and went out to see the cause of this wonder. There was Three Inch, climbing down from his tree.

"I have brought the eight thieves. Now may I marry the princess?"

The King was impressed by Three Inch. Though he was small and very ugly, he was clever and bold. Yes, he was a fitting husband for a princess.

On the wedding day a wondrous thing happened. Three Inch brought out the little flask of green liquid and rubbed it on the eyes of the princess. Her sight was restored. The kingdom rejoiced and the king felt sure he could not have found a better son-in-law anywhere in the world.

The father of Three Inch was freed from his slavery and Three Inch's parents came to live in the palace with their son. Though Three Inch remained small all of his life, his brave deeds had made him seem large in the hearts of his family.

Little Shell

A Visayan tale from the Philippines

*H*ere is yet another thumbling. But this one has better luck than most. A beautiful girl *wants* to marry him!

Do not be disgusted when he brings home a cow's head as a present for his mother. There is a lot of good meat on a cow's head.

In this tale, the thumbling has an especially close relationship with his mother. Without exception Little Shell gives the fruits of all of his dubious labors to his mother. And it is Little Shell's mother who goes, on her son's behalf, to the headman to ask for his daughter's hand in marriage. With the love of his mother and the love of his beautiful new wife Little Shell is transformed into a strong young man.

A man and his wife had one desire in life: to have a son. The woman prayed for a son. And at last she prayed, "I would like to have a son, even if he is no bigger than a seashell. Just grant me a son." A son was indeed born to this woman. But he was so very tiny. And as the years passed it became clear . . . he was never going to grow any larger than a seashell! So they called him Little Shell.

Little Shell's mother worried about him constantly for fear that something would happen to her small boy. But one day Little Shell asked her to let him go out alone.

"No. No. It is too dangerous. Some animal might swallow you, Little Shell."

"I am not afraid," said Little Shell. "It is time that I went out to help provide for my family."

So Little Shell set out. Wandering down the road he came to the stream. Several women were loading fish into their baskets. Little Shell crept quietly into one of the fish baskets. The woman picked it up and began to carry it up the road, not realizing that the tiny boy was hiding inside. When the woman passed near Little Shell's house he suddenly began to cry out "Run! Run!" The woman thought her basket had become bewitched. She dropped it and ran off as fast as she could. Little Shell climbed out of the basket, dragged it up the path, and presented the fish to his mother.

The next day Little Shell asked again if he might go out and search for food. "I don't know how you do it," said his mother. "But go if you will."

So Little Shell traveled along the road. Soon he saw a man carrying a cow's head. The man stopped for a moment to chat with a friend and leaned the cow's head against the fence. Little Shell saw his chance. He climbed right up and hid in the cow's ear. Soon the man picked up the cow's head, put it on his shoulder, and began walking down the road again. When he passed by Little Shell's house Little Shell began to shout. "Run! Run! Run!" The man thought the spirit of the cow had returned to haunt him. He threw down the cow's head and ran off up the road. Then Little Shell dragged the cow's head into his yard and called his mother. One can have much good food from a cow's head, so his mother was delighted.

Little Shell   93

Some time later Little Shell decided he wanted to get married. "Mother, go and ask the headman's daughter to be my wife," said Little Shell. "I hardly think so," said his mother. "She is not going to want to marry a small person like you." But Little Shell would not give up. At last the poor woman went trembling to the headman's house. "My son, Little Shell, asks to marry your daughter." The headman was astonished. He considered this a foolish request. "My daughter certainly will not agree to marry any person who is no bigger than a shell," he said. "But we will let her tell you herself." So the daughter was sent for. To everyone's amazement, the girl said, "Little Shell, I have seen him. He is small. But he is pleasant. I like that one. Yes, I will marry Little Shell."

The headman was furious. "If you marry such a creature you will not live in my village any longer."

The girl agreed to marry Little Shell anyway. The couple had to flee from the village to escape the angry father. They found a tiny house in the fields, and tried to find happiness there. But the girl did miss her family and friends.

However, after the first week, something wonderful began to happen. Little Shell had been under the enchantment of an evil spirit since he was born. The love of this beautiful girl slowly began to break the spell. Little Shell began to grow. Soon he had grown into a strong young man, as big as any. When the headman saw the fully grown Shell, he was embarrassed for his meanness. He forgave his daughter and the couple returned to the village to live in happiness the rest of their days.

Issun Boshi

A tale from Japan

This is one of Japan's most popular children's stories. The tiny little hero who defeats an ogre to win the princess never fails to delight children.

With its repetitive phrases, this story is perfect for audience participation storytelling. The imagery in this story is striking. A needle becomes a sword. A rice bowl becomes a boat. Chopsticks become oars. Armed with his frail equipment, Issun Boshi sets out to seek his fortune. He gets much more than he bargained for! Especially when he meets up with a Japanese feudal baron—the Daimyo.

*T*here was once an old man and an old woman who wanted a child so badly.
One day the couple went to the temple of Sumiyoshi-sama to pray.
"Sumiyoshi-sama, *please* give us a child.
We would love it and take such good care of it.
We would love it . . . even if it were no bigger . . .
. . . no bigger than the end of a finger."

The couple prayed for a very long time.
Then they returned to their home.

Do you know just ten months later . . .
a little baby was born to that couple!
But he was SO tiny.
He was only as big as the end of your finger.
Just *one inch long*.
So they called him *Issun Boshi*.
"Issun" means "one."
"Boshi" means "inch."
He was known as Little One Inch.

Issun Boshi was a darling tiny baby . . .
even though he was only one inch long.
But he never grew at all.
When he was one year old . . .
Issun Boshi was still one inch tall.
When he was two years old . . .
He was still . . . one inch tall.
When he was three years old . . .
He was still . . . one inch tall.
When he was four years old . . .
He was still . . . one inch tall.
When he was *ten* years old . . .
He was *still* . . . one inch tall!

And when Issun Boshi was twelve . . .
Yes, that boy was still just one inch tall.

But despite his tiny size, Issun Boshi wanted to go out and see the world.

"Okāsan, Otōsan . . . hear what I say," said Issun Boshi. "Mother and Father, I am
    ready to go out into the world."
"No. No. You are much too small," said his Mother.
"How would you defend yourself?"

"I must have a sword!" said Issun Boshi.
But his parents shook their heads.

"Where would we find a sword small enough for you, Little One Inch?"
Issun Boshi looked all around the house.
"Here is my sword!" he cried.
"Just give me my mother's needle!"

So his Mother prepared a little belt for Issun Boshi and he wore her needle at his
    waist like a real sword.

"I will need a boat," said Issun Boshi.
"Not possible," said his parents.
"Where would we find a boat small enough for you?"

Issun Boshi looked around the house.
"Here is my boat!" he cried.
"Give me a rice bowl for a boat!"

His Mother took down a rice bowl.
It was just the right size for Issun Boshi to ride in.

"Now for my oars," said Issun Boshi.
"But wherever can we find oars small enough for you, little Issun Boshi?" asked his
    parents.

Issun Boshi looked around the house.

"Here are my oars!" he cried.
"Just give me a pair of chopsticks!"

His parents gave him two small chopsticks.
They were just the thing to use as oars.

Issun Boshi's parents carried his rice bowl boat to the river.
Gently they set it on the water.
Tenderly they set little Issun Boshi inside the rice bowl.
They handed him his chopstick oars.
"Good-bye mother!
Good-bye father!
When you see me again, I will have made my fortune!"

Issun Boshi pushed off from the shore and began to row downstream.
"Good-bye little Issun Boshi!
Good luck!"

Issun Boshi rowed and rowed.
First to one side of the river . . .
then to the other . . .
Down the river he went.
And when he became tired he leaned on his chopstick oars and rested while the
    current carried him on.

At last his little boat reached the city.
"Here is where I shall make my fortune!" said Issun Boshi.
He pulled his boat to shore and jumped out.
What a lot of houses!
Issun Boshi wandered through the streets staring up at first one grand house and
    then another.
One house was larger and grander than all the others.
It was the home of a wealthy daimyo!
Issun Boshi went right up to this house and knocked at the door.
"Issun Boshi has come!

To offer his services!"
A servant opened the door.
But little Issun Boshi was standing beneath a wooden clog by the door.
The servant saw nothing at all.
A little voice called out.
"Issun Boshi has come!
To offer his services!"

The servant looked all around.
"Who is speaking?"

"It's me!
Here I am!
Look down!"

What a wonder!
The servant saw a little boy just one inch tall.
Issun Boshi was bowing respectfully.
"My name is Issun Boshi.
I would like to serve the Daimyo."

The servant carried Issun Boshi in and presented him to the daimyo.
"What a charming little creature!
He would make a fine playmate for my daughter.
Would you like that little Issun Boshi?"

"Indeed I would!"

So Issun Boshi became the companion of the great lord's daughter.
Everywhere she went, Issun Boshi accompanied her.
And what games they played!

They liked to play at flower cards.
Of course Issun Boshi could not hold the cards in his tiny hands,
but he would run up and down the table, lifting each card and peeking under to see
    what cards he had.

When his turn came to play, he would grab his card and *flip* it over.

The Princess liked to play at batting her shuttlecock around the yard.
Once Issun Boshi hid in the shuttlecock and got quite a ride.
He screamed with delight as he flew through the air. But he received quite a bruise on
    his leg when he landed.
The Princess forbade him to ever do such a thing again.

Of course Issun Boshi's favorite game was hide-and-seek, because he *always* won.

One day as the princess was making her visit to the shrine of Kannon-sama, an ogre
leaped from the forest and grabbed her up.

"Drop my friend at once!" demanded Issun Boshi.
"Let her go, or you shall suffer!"

The huge ogre was amused at the sight of this tiny boy, jumping about and challeng-
    ing him.
But Issun Boshi drew his needle sword,
leaped right onto the ogre's nose . . .
and began to stab that nose.

"OW! OW! Stop that!"

Issun Boshi wasn't through.
He jumped into the ogre's open mouth and
began to stab the poor ogre's tongue!

"OW! OW! OW!"
The ogre SPIT Issun Boshi out,
dropped the daimyo's daughter,
and ran bellowing off into the woods.
In his haste he dropped his magic golden hammer.

"Look!" cried Issun Boshi.
"The ogre has dropped his golden hammer.
These golden hammers are usually magic!

Quick, SHAKE it and make a wish!"
The daimyo's daughter picked up the golden hammer.
"What should I wish for . . ."
She looked at Issun Boshi.
She shook the golden hammer.
"I wish . . . that Issun Boshi would grow taller."

Issun Boshi felt his body begin to grow.
He was almost a foot tall now!
"I wish . . .that Issun Boshi would grow even taller."

Issun Boshi began to stretch and stretch . . .
He was three feet tall!

"I wish . . . that Issun Boshi would grow just a little taller."

Issun Boshi was now as tall as any other boy!

Do you know I am not sure,
but I think Issun Boshi stayed with that daimyo's daughter for a very long time.
I would not be at all surprised if they did not get married and live happily ever after.

Little Thumb Conquers the Sun

A tale from Myanmar (Burma)

I chose to retell this tale in a "tellable" format for storytellers. Its repetition and its spunky little hero create a fun story to share aloud. In this story a thumbling is inserted into a popular folktale type which usually settles on an animal as its main character. You might like to compare this story to "magic stomach" stories from other cultures. Several are listed in the notes to this tale on page 143.

There once was a boy so little that he stood only three inches tall.
Everyone called him Little Thumb.

One summer the sun shone with such heat that the garden
of Little Thumb's mother began to dry up.
The rice was dying.
All of the vegetables were dying.

"If the Sun does not stop this heat," said his mother,
"all of our rice and vegetables will die,
and we will have nothing to eat."

"Then the Sun must stop," said Little Thumb.
"I will go and tell him."

"Oh no, Little Thumb," said his mother.
"The Sun is so hot . . . he will burn you up."

"I may be small,
but I am brave!" said Little Thumb.
"I will go."

So his mother made Little Thumb a cake for his journey.
That cake was so large that Little Thumb had to carry it
    on his head!
But off he went, carrying his cake,
to meet the Sun.

Soon Little Thumb met a Boat.
"Hello, Little Thumb!" said the Boat.
"Where are you going with that cake on your head?"

"I am going to tell the Sun that he is TOO hot.
He is drying up my mother's garden."

"Can I go with you, Little Thumb?
I am so angry with that Sun.
Look at my river!

He has dried up all the water.
There is nowhere for me to float."

"Then come along," said Little Thumb.
"But first have a bite of my cake.
Then make yourself *very* tiny . . .
slip into my stomach . . .
and I will carry you there."

So Boat sat down and ate a bit of Little Thumb's cake.
"Mmm . . . mmm . . . mmm . . . mmm . . . ."
It was good.
Then Boat made himself *very* tiny . . ."Chink . . . chink!"
And . . ."Slip slide!"
He went inside.

Little Thumb traveled on his way.
After a while he met Bamboo Thorn.
"Hello, Little Thumb!" said Bamboo Thorn.
"Where are you going with that cake on your head?"

"I am going to tell the Sun that he is TOO hot.
He is drying up my mother's garden."

"Can I go with you, Little Thumb?
I am so angry with that Sun.
He has dried up all of my brother bamboos.
Just look how brown and dry they are."

"Then come along," said Little Thumb.
"But first have a bite of my cake.
Then make yourself *very* tiny . . .
slip into my stomach . . .
and I will carry you there."

So Bamboo Thorn sat down and ate a bit of Little Thumb's cake.
"Mmm . . . mmm . . . mmm . . . mmm . . . ."
It was good.

Then Bamboo Thorn made himself *very* tiny . . . "Chink . . . chink!"
and . . . "Slip slide!"
He went inside.

Little Thumb traveled on his way.
Next he met Clump of Moss.

"Hello, Little Thumb," said Clump of Moss.
"Where are you going with that piece of cake on your head?"

"I am going to tell the Sun that he is TOO hot.
He is drying up my mother's garden."

"Can I go with you, Little Thumb?
I am so angry with that Sun.
He has dried up all of my sister mosses.
Just look. They are brown and shriveled."

"Then come along," said Little Thumb.
"But first have a bite of my cake.
Then make yourself *very* tiny . . .
slip into my stomach . . .
and I will carry you there."

So Clump of Moss sat down and ate a bit of Little Thumb's cake.
"Mmm . . . mmm . . . mmm . . . mmm . . . ."
It was good.
Then Clump of Moss made herself *very* tiny . . . "Chink . . . chink!"
and . . . "Slip slide!"
She went inside.

Little Thumb traveled on his way.
Last of all he met Rotten Egg.
"Hello, Little Thumb," said Rotten Egg.
"Where are you going with that piece of cake on your head?"

"I am going to tell the Sun that he is TOO hot.
He is drying up my mother's garden!"

"Can I go with you, Little Thumb?
I am so angry with that Sun.
His heat has caused all the little chicks to die.
Only I, Rotten Egg, am left."

"Then come along," said Little Thumb.
"But first have a bite of my cake.
Then make yourself *very* tiny . . .
slip into my stomach . . .
and I will carry you there."

So Rotten Egg sat down and ate the last of Little Thumb's cake.
"Mmm . . . mmm . . . mmm . . . mmm . . . ."
It was good.
Then Rotten Egg made himself very tiny . . . "Chink . . . chink!"
and . . . "Slip slide!"
He went inside.

Little Thumb traveled on his way.
By nightfall he had reached the Northern Mountain.
"Here is where I stop," said Little Thumb.
"In the morning Sun will rise over Northern Mountain.
In the morning I will tell him he is TOO hot.

But where can I sleep tonight?"

High on the mountainside stood a house.
"I can sleep there," said Little Thumb.
"But I am afraid any house in such a deserted place
must belong to ogres."

Little Thumb crept up to the house and peered in the windows.
Sure enough, it was the house of an ogre.
But the ogre was nowhere in sight.

"I will have to sleep there," said Little Thumb.
"Maybe the ogre will not return."
But suddenly he heard a commotion in his stomach.

"Let us out! We can help!
Let us out! We will protect you!"

It was Bamboo Thorn, Clump of Moss, and Rotten Egg.
So Little Thumb opened his mouth and
"Slip hop!" out came Bamboo Thorn.
"Slip hop!" out came Clump of Moss.
"Slip hop!" out came Rotten Egg.

"You curl up in a corner and rest," said the three.
"We will guard the house while you sleep."

Little Thumb curled up in a corner and fell asleep.
Rotten Egg rolled over and hid himself among the ashes in the fireplace.
Clump of Moss spread herself out on the floor by the water jar.
And Bamboo Thorn hid under the ogre's bed.
Then they waited.

In the middle of the night the ogre came home.
He bashed open the door.
"PHEW! It smells like HUMAN in here!
PHEW! That's impossible."
He flung himself into his bed.
Soon he was snoring, sound asleep.

Then Bamboo Thorn began to do his work.
He drew out his long thorns and began to poke them up through the ogre's bed.
"Stick stick! Stick stick!
Stick stick! Stick stick!"

"Ouch! Something is *biting* me!"
The ogre flopped over onto his stomach.

"Stick stick! Stick stick!
Stick stick! Stick stick!"
"OWWW! This bed has bugs!"

The ogre jumped up and ran to the fireplace to light his lamp.
Rotten Egg was ready.

When the ogre leaned over to get a light, Rotten Egg exploded!

Ashes flew into the ogre's eyes!

He couldn't see anything.

"AAACK!"

The ogre ran to the water jar to wash his eyes.

But Clump of Moss was ready for him.

She spread herself right in his path and

"SLIIIIIP! CRASH!"

That ogre slipped on Clump of Moss and fell to the ground with such a whack that he knocked himself dead.

"Wake up, Little Thumb!" cried the three friends.

"The ogre is dead.

You can sleep in his bed!"

So Little Thumb had a good night's sleep.

And in the morning, when the Sun rose,

Little Thumb and his companions were waiting on top of Northern Mountain.

Here came the Sun.

Slowly at first . . . lifting his rosy head.

"SUN!" called Little Thumb.

"We have come to tell you. You are TOO hot!

You are drying up my mother's garden!"

"Yes," said Bamboo Thorn.

"And you are drying up all of my brother bamboos!"

"And my sister mosses!" added Clump of Moss.

"And you have caused all the little chicks to die!" shouted Rotten Egg.

"You are TOO hot!" shouted the companions all together.

When Sun heard this he became angry.

He began to glow and glow . . .

hotter and hotter . . .

as the anger rose in him.

Poor Little Thumb felt that great heat.

Bamboo Thorn and Clump of Moss began to shrivel.

Rotten Egg and Little Thumb were drying up too.

The friends were about to be defeated.

But suddenly someone came to their aid.

It was RAIN!

Rain is Sun's old enemy.

When Rain saw brave Little Thumb challenging Sun he came rushing across the sky to help.

That Rain flew in Sun's face and dampened all his heat.

Rain poured and poured.

Little Thumb and his companions were saved.

"Thank you, Rain!" called Little Thumb.

Rain poured and poured.

"Thank you, Rain!" called Bamboo Thorn.

Rain poured and poured.

"Thank you, Rain!" called Clump of Moss.

Rain poured and poured.

"Thank you, Rain!" called Rotten Egg.

Rain poured and poured.

"Oh NO!" realized Little Thumb.

"Now I think we are going to DROWN!"

The water was coming higher and higher.

But just then . . .

"Is it MY turn to help?" called a voice from inside Little Thumb's stomach.

"Don't forget ME."

It was BOAT.

Little Thumb opened his mouth and "Slip hop!"

Out came Boat.

Just in time.

Boat made himself large again.

Little Thumb, Bamboo Thorn, Clump of Moss, and Rotten Egg all climbed inside.

Then Boat carried them all safely home to Little Thumb's mother.

That is the tale of how Little Thumb went to conquer the Sun.

Thumbling the Giant

A German tale from the Brothers Grimm

A thumbling transformed into a giant? Despite the contradiction in terms, that's exactly what happens to the thumbling in this tale by the Brothers Grimm.

Thanks to good nutrition and the loving care of a giant who raises him, Thumbling grows and grows and grows. Although clever and resourceful (as all thumblings are!), this giant thumbling faces some unique challenges as he tries to make his way in the world without wreaking too much havoc on the people he encounters. He returns home to astonish his birth parents, then goes to work for a farmer. His wages? He is allowed to give the farmer two strokes on the shoulder every fortnight. This tale is full of wonder at the things a *huge* person can do.

Once upon a time there lived a husbandman who had a son who, when he was born, was no bigger than the length of a thumb, and who for many years did not grow a hair's breadth taller.

One morning, just as the countryman was about to set out to plow his field, little Thumbling said:

"Father, I want to go, too."

"I dare say you do," said the man; "but you are much better at home. If I took you out I should be sure to lose you."

Thereupon Thumbling fell a-crying, and cried so much that at length his father picked him up and put him in his pocket and set forth to his work.

When they reached the fields the man took his son out and set him down on the ridge of a newly turned furrow, so that he might see the world around him. Then suddenly from over the mountains a great giant came striding toward them.

"See, son," said the husbandman, "here is an ogre coming to fetch you away because you were naughty and cried this morning."

And the words had scarcely passed his lips when, in two great strides, the giant had reached little Thumbling's side and had picked him up in his great hands and carried him away without uttering a sound.

The poor father stood dumb with fear, for he thought he should never see his little son again.

The giant, however, treated little Thumbling very kindly in his house in the woods. He kept him warm in his pocket, and fed him so heartily and well that Thumbling became a young giant himself, tall, and broad.

At the end of two years the old giant took him out into the woods to try his strength.

"Pull up that birch-tree for a staff to lean upon," he said, and the youth obeyed and pulled it up by the roots as if it had been a mere weed.

The old giant still thought he should like him to be stronger, so, after taking great care of him for another two years, they again went out into the wood. This time Thumbling playfully uprooted a stout old oak, and the old giant, well pleased, cried:

"Now you are a credit to me," and took him back to the field where he first found him.

Here the young giant's father happened to be just then plowing; so Thumbling went up to him and said:

"See, father, to what a great big man your son has grown!"

But the peasant was afraid.

"Be off with you! I don't know you," he cried.

"But really and truly, father, I am your son," he said.

"Let me take the plow, for I can guide it quite as well as you."

The father very unwillingly let go of the plow, for he was afraid of the giant, and sat down to watch. Then Thumbling laid one hand on the plowshare and straightway drove it so deep into the ground that the peasant cried:

"Now you will do more harm than good, if you drive so deep into the earth."

Thereupon the young giant unharnessed the horses and began to draw the plow himself, first saying:

"Now, father, get you home and tell mother to cook a hearty meal, while I just run round the field."

And in a very short time he had done what the peasant would have taken two whole days to do.

When all was finished, he laid plow, horse, and harrow over his shoulders and carried them home as easily as though they were a truss of hay.

When he reached the house, he saw his mother sitting on a bench in the courtyard.

"Oh, who is this frightful monster of a man?" she cried.

"That is our son," said her husband.

"I cannot believe that," replied the woman, "for our child was a tiny little thing," and she begged the young giant to go away.

However, he did not take any notice of what she said, for, after feeding the horse in the stable, he came into the kitchen and sat himself down upon the edge of the dresser.

"Mother, mother," he said, "I am so hungry. Give me my dinner."

"Here it is," said his mother, and set two enormous dishes of smoking stew upon the table.

It would have been enough to last the husbandman and his wife for eight whole days, but the giant ate it all up in five minutes, and then asked if they could give him more. But the woman shook her head, and said they had no more in the house.

"Mother," he said, "I am fainting with hunger. That was a mere bite."

The woman was so frightened at this that she ran and made some more stew in the largest fish kettle.

"Ah," sighed the young giant, "this is something like a meal!"

But when he had finished he still felt hungry, and said:

"Well, father, I can see I shall starve if I come here to live. I will go and seek my fortune in the wide world, if you can procure me a bar of iron so strong that I cannot break it across my knee."

The peasant quickly harnessed his two horses to the wagon, and from the smithy in the village he fetched an iron bar so heavy that the horses could hardly drag it. This the giant tried across his knee. Snap! it cracked in half, like a twig.

Then the peasant took his wagon and four horses to the smithy and brought back as heavy a bar as they could carry. But in a second the giant had broken it into two pieces and tossed them each aside.

"Father," he said, "I need a stronger one yet. Take the wagon and eight horses to the smithy, and fetch me back as heavy a one as they can draw."

This the countryman did, and again the youth broke it in two as easily as if he had cracked a nut.

"Well, father, I see you cannot get me anything strong enough. I must go and try my fortune without it."

So he turned blacksmith and journeyed for many miles, until he came to a village, where dwelt a very grasping smith, who earned a great deal of money, but who gave not a penny of it away.

The giant stepped into his forge and asked if by any chance he were in want of help.

"What wages do you ask?" said the smith, looking the young man up and down; for, thought he: "Here is a fine, powerful fellow, who surely will be worth his salt."

"I don't want money," replied the giant. "But here's a bargian: every fortnight, when you give your workmen their wages, I will give you two strokes across your shoulders. It will be just a little amusement for me."

The cunning smith agreed very willingly, for, he thought, in this way he would save a great deal of money.

However, next morning when the new journeyman started work, with the very first stroke he gave the red-hot iron, it shivered into a thousand pieces, and the anvil buried itself so deep in the earth that he could not pull it out again.

"Here, fellow," cried his master, "you won't suit me; you are far too clumsy. I must put an end to our bargain."

"Just as you please," said the other, "but you must pay me for the work I have done, so I will just give you one little tap on the shoulder."

With that he gave the greedy smith such a blow that it knocked him flying over four hay-ricks. Then, picking up the stoutest iron bar he could find for a walking-stick, he set forth once more on his travels.

Presently he came to a farmhouse, where he inquired if they were in need of a bailiff. Now, the farmer just happened to need a head man, so he was engaged at once upon the same terms as he had arranged with the old blacksmith.

Next morning the farm servants were to go and fell trees in the wood, but just as they were ready to start they found the new bailiff was still in bed and fast asleep.

They shook him and shouted at him, but he would not open his eyes; he only grumbled at them and told them to be gone.

"I shall have done my work and reached home long before you," he said.

So he stayed in bed another two hours, then arose, and after eating a hearty breakfast he started with his cart and horses for the wood.

There was a narrow pathway through which he had to pass just before entering the wood, and after he had led his horses through this he went back and built up a barrier of brambles and furze and branches so thick that no horse could possibly force its way through.

Then he drove on and met his fellow-servants just leaving the wood on their way home.

"Drive on, my friends," he said, "and I will be home before you even now."

Then he pulled up a giant elm by its roots just on the border of the woods, and laying it on his cart, he turned and quickly overtook the others.

There they were, staring helplessly at the great barricade which barred their path, just as he had expected to find them.

"Ha, ha!" he chuckled, "you might just as well have slept an hour or two longer, for I told you you would not get home before me."

Then, shouldering the tree, the horse and the cart, he pushed a way through the barrier as easily as if he had been carrying a bag of feathers.

When he got back to the farm he showed his new walking-stick, as he called the tree, to his master.

"Wife," said the farmer, "we have indeed found a capital bailiff, and if he does need more sleep than the others, he works much better."

So the months rolled by, until a whole year had come and gone, and the time had arrived to pay the servants their wages. But the farmer was overcome with fright when he remembered the blows the giant had to give him. So he begged him to change his mind and accept his whole farm and lands instead.

"No," said the giant, "I am a bailiff, and a bailiff I intend to remain, so you must pay me the wages we agreed upon."

The farmer now obtained a promise that he would give him a fortnight to think the matter over, and he secretly assembled all his friends and neighbors to discuss what he should do.

The only thing they could suggest was to slay the bailiff, and it was arranged that he should be told to bring a cartload of millstones to the edge of the well, and then the farmer was to send him down to the bottom to clean it out. When the giant was safely at the bottom, all the friends and neighbors would come and roll the millstones down upon him.

Everything happened as had been planned, and when the bailiff was at the bottom of the well the millstones were rolled in. As each one fell, the water splashed over the top in a great wave.

It seemed impossible that the bailiff should not be crushed to death, but suddenly the neighbors heard him call out:

"I say, you up there, shoo away the chickens; they are scattering the gravel in my eyes!"

Then he quickly finished his task, and presently jumped out of the well with one of the millstones hanging round his neck.

"Have not I got a handsome collar?" he said.

Again the farmer was overcome with fear, and again he called together all his friends and relations. The only thing they could think of was to advise the farmer to send the bailiff to the haunted mill by night, and order him to grind eight bushels of corn. "For," said they, "no man who has spent a night there has ever come out alive."

So the bailiff went and fetched the corn from the loft. He put two bushels in his right-hand pocket, and two in his left, and the rest he carried in a sack across his shoulders.

When he reached the mill the miller told him it was haunted, and he had best come to grind his corn in the daytime if he did not wish to lose his life.

"Tush, tush!" said the giant. "Make haste and leave me alone. Come back in the morning, and I promise you will find me all safe and sound."

Then he entered the mill and emptied his sacks into the hopper, and by twelve o'clock he had finished his work. Feeling a little weary, he sat down to rest, but noticed with great interest the door opening very slowly, all by itself.

Then a table laden with rich food and wines came and set itself before him. Still there was no living creature to be seen. Next the chairs came and placed themselves round the festive board, and then he noticed fingers handling the knives and forks and placing food upon the plates.

The giant soon got tired of watching this, and as he felt quite ready for a meal himself, he drew up his chair to the table and partook of a hearty repast.

Just as he finished he felt a breath of air blow out all the lights, and then a thundering blow fell upon his head.

"Well, I'm not going to put up with this," he said. "If I feel any more taps like that one I will just tap back."

Then a great battle raged, and blows fell thickly all around, but he never let himself feel any fear, but only gave back as many as he could.

When morning came the miller hastened to the mill expecting to find the giant dead, but he was greeted with a hearty laugh.

"Well, miller," said the giant, "somebody has been slapping me in the night, but I guess they have had as good blows as they have given, and I have managed to eat a hearty supper into the bargain."

The miller was overjoyed to find the evil spell had been broken, and begged the giant to accept some money as reward, but this he refused. Slinging the meal on his shoulders, he went back to ask his wages from the farmer.

The farmer was furious to see his bailiff safe and sound again, and paced his floor to and fro, shivering and shaking like a leaf. He felt he could not breathe, so he threw the window open, and before he knew what had happened the giant had sent him flying out of the window straight over the hills into Nowhere Land. And as the farmer had not waited to receive the second stroke, the giant gave it to his wife, and she flew out to join her husband, and for aught I know they are flying through the air still.

Tough Little Niraidak

An Evenk tale from Siberia

In this Evenk tale, a spunky wee fellow challenges the world and remains self-confident and happy, despite its rebuffs. This tale is full of imagery that fuels the imagination and brings the tiny character to life.

Niraidak finds his size to be an asset, not a liability, until he must provide a home and food for his new wife. Despite his best efforts, he is unable to meet her demands. Although the marriage fails, Niraidak is philosophical. "What shall we do next?" he asks his faithful deer.

Once in the early days, there lived a tiny man named Niraidak.

This fellow was so small that his tent was made of eight twigs from a rose willow and three squirrel skins.

He was so tiny that his coat was made of two sable skins, his hat of a single mole skin, and his mittens each from the skin of one mouse.

Niraidak had a deer bone knife and a small deer on whose back he could ride when he hunted.

When he killed a squirrel or a mouse or a small bird, it was as if a grown man should kill a fox or a rabbit or a giant eagle.

Since Niraidak lived alone, he had no one else to compare himself with.

It seemed to tiny Niraidak that he was a strong and mighty hunter.

So one day he set off to have adventures.

"Come friend deer," he said.

"I will ride into the wide world and defeat all the giants!

I will ride into the wide world and choose myself a bride!"

He mounted his magic saddle deer and spoke to it,

"Change . . . change . . . into a fire-breathing boar and away we will go!"

Off they raced.

Little Niraidak sat on the boar's back and sang a merry song as they ran.

If anyone got in their way, the boar would snort his fire at them and pierce them with his sharp tusks and trample them with his heavy hoofs.

While all the time Niraidak sat firmly on the boar's back, not concerned in the least.

At last he reached the home of the giant Dioloni, the Man of Stone.

"Time for ACTION!" called Niraidak.

His boar turned back into a deer, and Niraidak hopped to the ground.

He ran for the giant Dioloni's back, making his shrill war cry.

But just as he reached the giant he tripped and bumped his nose on the heel of the giant's foot.

"Huh?" Dioloni turned around.

"What is this little thing?"

Dioloni plucked Niraidak from the ground as you would pluck up a beetle.

"I am the mighty Niraidak!

I have come to slay you!"

Niraidak began to leap around on the giant's palm, making stabbing motions in the air.

"Huh?" Dioloni picked Niraidak up and stuffed him into his jacket.

Little Niraidak was not daunted, but he saw that the battle here was useless.

He slid quietly down the giant's sleeve, dropped to the ground, and leaped back onto his deer.

"So much for the giants,

Let's go look for the beautiful maiden!"

Off they went, riding swiftly over the terrain.

"You'd better not be here when I come back," he called over his shoulder to Dioloni.

"I'll skin you alive and trample you to dust!"

Soon they reached the village of beautiful women.

Each was lovelier than the last.

Niraidak lined them all up.

He went down the line examining each woman carefully.

"This is the most beautiful," he said.

"She is the bride for me!"

And with the beautiful woman riding the deer in front of him he raced off home.

But when they arrived at his little tent, Niraidak saw that it would not do.

The tiny twig and squirrel skin tent would not even cover his wife's feet.

So he set about to build a larger tent for his new bride.

When the tent was ready, Niraidak left his wife there and went off to catch fish for their meal.

He caught 25 tiny fish and was so proud of himself.

But when he had strung them on a twig, he realized that this burden was too heavy for him to carry.

So Niraidak went back to the tent to fetch his wife.

"Come help carry my catch, wife.

I have caught so many fish that I cannot carry them alone!

See what a great provider you have married!"

When his wife arrived at the riverbank and saw the 25 tiny minnows strung on the willow twig she was furious.

"You expect THIS to be my meal!

It's hardly a mouthful!"

She carried the twig home in one hand, cooked the fish, and ate them.

She was as hungry as before she started.

"Never mind," said Niraidak.

"Put this stone on your stomach.

Then you won't feel so hungry."

And he went off to search for more food.

As soon as he was gone, his wife packed her things and left.

"This is no husband for me," she said.

"I would soon starve with nothing to eat but minnows."

And off she went to a place where strong, husky hunters could be found.

Tiny Niraidak was not surprised to find her gone when he returned.

"What a job it would have been to keep her fed!" he said.

And jumping on his deer he rode off, singing happily in his tiny voice.

"I've fought the giant and married the beautiful woman," he said to his deer.

"What shall we do next?"

Thumbelina

A tale by Danish author Hans Christian Andersen

Here is Hans Christian Andersen's "Thumbelina." Andersen begins his story much like other thumbling tales. A woman wishes for a child, even if no larger than her thumb. But immediately Andersen's imagination takes over the story and the simple folktale disappears into his extraordinary fairyland. Enjoy the elaborate descriptions of Andersen's tale, then compare this to a simple folk version such as the Brothers Grimm version of "Thumbling."

There was once a woman who wanted to have quite a tiny, little child, but she did not know where to get one from. So one day she went to an old Witch and said to her: "I should so much like to have a tiny, little child; can you tell me where I can get one?"

"Oh, we have just got one ready!" said the Witch. "Here is a barley-corn for you, but it's not the kind the farmer sows in his field, or feeds the cocks and hens with, I can tell you. Put it in a flowerpot, and then you will see something happen."

"Oh, thank you!" said the woman, and gave the Witch a shilling, for that was what it cost. Then she went home and planted the barley-corn; immediately there grew out of it a large and beautiful flower, which looked like a tulip, but the petals were tightly closed as if it were still only a bud.

"What a beautiful flower!" exclaimed the woman, and she kissed the red and yellow petals; but as she kissed them the flower burst open. It was a real tulip, such as one can see any day; but in the middle of the blossom, on the green velvety petals, sat a little girl, quite tiny, trim, and pretty. She was scarcely half a thumb in height; so they called her Thumbelina. An elegant polished walnut-shell served Thumbelina as a cradle, the blue petals of a violet were her mattress, and a rose-leaf her coverlid. There she lay at night, but in the day-time she  used to play about on the table; here the woman had put a bowl, surrounded by a ring of flowers, with their stalks in water, in the middle of which floated a great tulip pedal, and on this Thumbelina sat, and sailed from one side of the bowl to the other, rowing herself with two white horse-hairs for oars. It was such a pretty sight! She could sing, too, with a voice more soft and sweet than had ever been heard before.

One night, when she was lying in her pretty little bed, an old toad crept in through a broken pane in the window. She was very ugly, clumsy, and clammy; she hopped on to the table where Thumbelina lay asleep under the red rose-leaf.

"This would make a beautiful wife for my son," said the toad, taking up the walnut-shell, with Thumbelina inside, and hopping with it through the window into the garden.

There flowed a great wide stream, with slippery and marshy banks; here the toad lived with her son. Ugh! how ugly and clammy he was, just like his mother! "Croak, croak, croak!" was all he could say when he saw the pretty little girl in the walnut-shell.

"Don't talk so loud, or you'll wake her," said the old toad. "She might escape us even now; she is as light as a feather. We will put her at once on a broad water-lily leaf in the stream. That will be quite an island for her; she is so small and light. She can't run away from us there, whilst we are preparing the guest-chamber under the marsh where she shall live."

Outside in the brook grew many water-lilies, with broad green leaves, which looked as if they were swimming about on the water. The leaf farthest away was the largest, and to this the old toad swam with Thumbelina in her walnut-shell.

The tiny Thumbelina woke up very early in the morning, and when she saw where she was she began to cry bitterly; for on every side of the great green leaf was water, and she could not get to the land.

The old toad was down under the marsh, decorating her room with rushes and yellow marigold leaves, to make it very grand for her new daughter-in-law; then she swam out with her ugly son to the leaf where Thumbelina lay. She wanted to fetch the pretty cradle to put it into her room before Thumbelina herself came there. The old toad bowed low in the water before her, and said: "Here is my son; you shall marry him, and live in great magnificence down under the marsh."

"Croak, croak, croak!" was all the son could say. Then they took the neat little cradle and swam away with it. Thumbelina sat alone on the great green leaf and wept, for she did not want to live with the toad or marry her ugly son. The little fishes swimming about under the water had seen the toad quite plainly and heard what she had said. They put up their heads to see the little girl, and thought her so pretty they were very sorry she should go down with the ugly toad to live. No, that must not happen. They assembled in the water round the green stalk which supported the leaf on which she was sitting and nibbled the stem in two. Away floated the leaf down the stream, bearing Thumbelina far beyond the reach of the toad.

On she sailed past several towns, and the little birds sitting in the bushes saw her, and sang, "What a pretty little girl!" The leaf floated farther and farther away; thus Thumbelina left her native land.

A beautiful little white butterfly fluttered above her, and at last settled on the leaf. Thumbelina pleased him, and she, too, was delighted, for now the toads could not reach her, and it was so beautiful where she was travelling; the sun shone on the water and made it sparkle like the brightest silver. She took off her sash, and tied one end round the butterfly; the other end she fastened to the leaf, so that now it glided along with her faster than ever.

A great cockchafer came flying past; he caught sight of Thumbelina, and in a moment had put his arms round her slender waist, and had flown off with her to a tree. The green leaf floated away down the stream, and the butterfly with it, for he was fastened to the leaf and could not get loose from it. Oh, dear! how terrified poor little Thumbelina was when the cockchafer flew off with her to the tree! But she was especially distressed on the beautiful white butterfly's account, as she had tied him fast, so that if he could not get away he must starve to death. But the cockchafer did not trouble himself about that; he sat down with her on a large green leaf, gave her the honey out of the flowers to eat, and told her that she was very pretty, although she wasn't in the least like a cockchafer. Later on, all the other cockchafers who lived in the same tree came to pay calls; they examined Thumbelina closely, and remarked, "Why, she has only two legs! How very miserable!"

"She has no feelers!" cried another.

"How ugly she is!" said all the lady chafers—and yet Thumbelina was really very pretty.

The cockchafer who had stolen her knew this very well; but when he heard all the ladies saying she was ugly, he began to think so too, and would not keep her; she might go wherever she liked. So he flew down from the tree with her and put her on a daisy. There she sat and wept, because she was so ugly that the cockchafer would have nothing to do with her; and yet she was the most beautiful creature imaginable, so soft and delicate, like the loveliest rose-leaf.

The whole summer poor little Thumbelina lived alone in the great wood. She plaited a bed for herself of blades of grass, and hung it up under a clover-leaf, so that she was protected from the rain; she gathered honey from the flowers for food, and drank the dew on the leaves every morning. Thus the summer and autumn passed, but then came winter—the long, cold winter. All the birds who had sung so sweetly about her had flown away; the trees shed their leaves, the flowers died; the great clover-leaf under which she had lived curled up, and nothing remained of it but the withered stalk. She was terribly cold, for her clothes were ragged, and she herself was so small and thin. Poor little Thumbelina! she would surely be frozen to death. It began to snow, and every snow-flake that fell on her was to her as a whole shovelful thrown on one of us, for we are so big, and she was only an inch high. She wrapt herself round in a dead leaf, but it was torn in the middle and gave her no warmth; she was trembling with cold.

Just outside the wood where she was now living lay a great corn-field. But the corn had been gone a long time; only the dry, bare stubble was left standing in the frozen ground. This made a forest for her to wander about in. All at once she came across the door of a field-mouse, who had a little hole under a corn-stalk. There the mouse lived warm and snug, with a store-room full of corn, a splendid kitchen and dining-room. Poor little Thumbelina went up to the door and begged for a little piece of barley, for she had not had anything to eat for the last two days.

"Poor little creature!" said the field-mouse, for she was a kind-hearted old thing at the bottom. "Come into my warm room and have some dinner with me."

As Thumbelina pleased her, she said: "As far as I am concerned you may spend the winter with me; but you must keep my room clean and tidy, and tell me stories, for I like that very much."

And Thumbelina did all that the kind old field-mouse asked, and did it remarkably well too.

"Now I am expecting a visitor," said the field-mouse; "my neighbour comes to call on me once a week. He is in better circumstances than I am, has great, big rooms, and wears a fine black-velvet coat. If you could only marry him, you would be well provided for. But he is blind. You must tell him all the prettiest stories you know."

But Thumbelina did not trouble her head about him, for he was only a mole. He came and paid them a visit in his black-velvet coat.

"He is so rich and so accomplished," the field mouse told her. "His house is twenty times larger than mine; he possesses great knowledge, but he cannot bear the sun and the beautiful flowers, and speaks slightingly of them, for he has never seen them."

Thumbelina had to sing to him, so she sang "Lady-bird, lady-bird, fly away home!" and other songs so prettily that the mole fell in love with her; but he did not say anything, he was a very cautious man. A short time before he had dug a long passage through the ground from his own house to that of his neighbour; in this he gave the field-mouse and Thumbelina permission to walk as often as they liked. But he begged them not to be afraid of the dead bird that lay in the passage: it was a real bird with beak and feathers, and must have died a little time ago, and now laid buried just where he had made his tunnel. The mole took a piece of rotten wood in his mouth, for that glows like fire in the dark, and went in front, lighting them through the long dark passage. When they came to the place where the dead bird lay, the mole put his broad nose against the ceiling and pushed a hole through, so that the daylight could shine down. In the middle of the path lay a dead swallow, his pretty wings pressed close to his sides, his claws and head drawn under his feathers; the poor bird had evidently died of cold. Thumbelina was very sorry, for she was very fond of all little birds; they had sung and twittered so beautifully to her all through the summer. But the mole kicked him with his bandy legs and said:

"Now he can't sing any more! It must be very miserable to be a little bird! I'm thankful that none of my little children are; birds always starve in winter."

"Yes, you speak like a sensible man," said the field-mouse. "What has a bird, in spite of all his singing, in the winter-time? He must starve and freeze, and that must not be very pleasant for him, I must say!"

Thumbelina did not say anything; but when the other two had passed on she bent down to the bird, brushed aside the feathers from his head, and kissed his closed eyes gently. "Perhaps it was he that sang to me so prettily in the summer," she thought. "How much pleasure he did give me, dear little bird!"

The mole closed up the hole again which let in the light, and then escorted the ladies home. But Thumbelina could not sleep that night; so she got out of bed, and plaited a great big blanket of straw, and carried it off, and spread it over the dead bird, and piled upon it thistle-down as soft as cotton-wool, which she had found in the field-mouse's room, so that the poor little thing should lie warmly buried.

"Farewell, pretty little bird!" she said. "Farewell, and thank you for your beautiful songs in the summer, when the trees were green, and the sun shone down warmly on us!" Then she laid her head against the bird's heart. But the bird was not dead: he had been frozen, but now that she had warmed him, he was coming to life again.

In autumn the swallows fly away to foreign lands; but there are some who are late in starting, and then they get so cold that they drop down as if dead, and the snow comes and covers them over.

Thumbelina trembled, she was so frightened; for the bird was very large in comparison with herself—only an inch high. But she took courage, piled up the down more closely over the poor swallow, fetched her own coverlid and laid it over his head.

Next night she crept out again to him. There he was alive, but very weak; he could only open his eyes for a moment and look at Thumbelina, who was standing in front of him with a piece of rotten wood in her hand, for she had no other lantern.

"Thank you, pretty little child!" said the swallow to her. "I am so beautifully warm! Soon I shall regain my strength, and then I shall be able to fly out again into the warm sunshine."

Oh! she said, "it is very cold outside; it is snowing and freezing! stay in your warm bed; I will take care of you!"

Then she brought him water in a petal, which he drank, after which he related to her how he had torn one of his wings on a bramble, so that he could not fly as fast as the other swallows, who had flown far away to warmer lands. So at last he had dropped down exhausted, and then he could remember no more. The whole winter he remained down there, and Thumbelina looked after him and nursed him tenderly. Neither the mole nor the field-mouse learnt anything of this, for they could not bear the poor swallow.

When the spring came, and the sun warmed the earth again, the swallow said farewell to Thumbelina, who opened the hole in the roof for him which the mole had made. The sun shone brightly down upon her, and the swallow asked her if she would go with him; she could sit upon his back. Thumbelina wanted very much to fly far away into the green wood, but she knew that the old field-mouse would be sad if she ran away. "No, I mustn't come!" she said.

"Farewell, dear good little girl!" said the swallow, and flew off into the sunshine. Thumbelina gazed after him with the tears standing in her eyes, for she was very fond of the swallow.

"Tweet, tweet!" sang the bird, and flew into the green wood. Thumbelina was very unhappy. She was not allowed to go out into the warm sunshine. The corn which had been sowed in the field over the field-mouse's home grew up high into the air, and made a thick forest for the poor little girl, who was only an inch high.

"Now you are to be a bride, Thumbelina!" said the field-mouse, "for our neighbour has proposed for you! What a piece of fortune for a poor child like you! Now you must set to work at your linen for your dowry, for nothing must be lacking if you are to become the wife of our neighbour, the mole!"

Thumbelina had to spin all day long, and every evening the mole visited her, and told her that when the summer was over the sun would not shine so hot; now it was burning the earth as hard as a stone. Yes, when the summer had passed, they would keep the wedding.

But she was not at all pleased about it, for she did not like the stupid mole. Every morning when the sun was rising, and every evening when it was setting, she would steal out of the house-door, and when the breeze parted the ears of corn so that she could see the blue sky through them, she thought how bright and beautiful it must be outside, and longed to see her dear swallow again. But he never came; no doubt he had flown away far into the great green wood.

By the autumn Thumbelina had finished the dowry.

"In four weeks you will be married!" said the field-mouse; "don't be obstinate, or I shall bite you with my sharp white teeth! You will get a fine husband! The King himself has not such a velvet coat. His store-room and cellar are full, and you should be thankful for that."

Well, the wedding-day arrived. The mole had come to fetch Thumbelina to live with him deep down under the ground, never to come out into the warm sun again, for that was what he didn't like. The poor little girl was very sad; for now she must say goodbye to the beautiful sun.

"Farewell, bright sun!" she cried, stretching out her arms towards it, and taking another step outside the house; for now the corn had been reaped, and only the dry stubble was left standing. "Farewell, farewell!" she said, and put her arms round a little red flower that grew there. "Give my love to the dear swallow when you see him!"

"Tweet, tweet!" sounded in her ear all at once. She looked up. There was the swallow flying past! As soon as he saw Thumbelina, he was very glad. She told him how unwilling she was to marry the ugly mole, as then she had to live underground where the sun never shone, and she could not help bursting into tears.

"The cold winter is coming now," said the swallow. "I must fly away to warmer lands: will you come with me? You can sit on my back, and we will fly far away from the ugly mole and his dark house, over the mountains, to the warm countries where the sun shines more brightly than here, where it is always summer, and there are always beautiful flowers. Do come with me, dear little Thumbelina, who saved my life when I lay frozen in the dark tunnel!"

"Yes, I will go with you," said Thumbelina, and got on the swallow's back, with her feet on one of his outstretched wings. Up he flew into the air, over woods and seas, over the great mountains where the snow is always lying. And if she was cold she crept under his warm feathers, only keeping her little head out to admire all the beautiful things in the world beneath. At last they came to warm lands; there the sun was brighter, the sky seemed twice as high, and in the hedges hung the finest green and purple grapes; in the woods grew oranges and lemons: the air was scented with myrtle and mint, and on the roads were pretty little children running about and playing with great gorgeous butterflies. But the swallow flew on farther, and it became more and more beautiful. Under the most splendid green trees besides a blue lake stood a glittering white-marble castle. Vines hung about the high pillars; there were many swallows' nests, and in one of these lived the swallow who was carrying Thumbelina.

"Here is my house!" said he. "But it won't do for you to live with me; I am not tidy enough to please you. Find a home for yourself in one of the lovely flowers that grow down there; now I will set you down, and you can do whatever you like."

"That will be splendid!" said she, clapping her little hands.

There lay a great white marble column which had fallen to the ground and broken into three pieces, but between these grew the most beautiful white flowers. The swallow flew down with Thumbelina, and set her upon one of the broad leaves. But there, to her astonishment, she found a tiny little man sitting in the middle of the flower, as white and transparent as if he were made of glass; he had the prettiest golden crown on his head, and the most beautiful wings on his shoulders; he himself was no bigger than Thumbelina. He was the spirit of the flower. In each blossom there dwelt a tiny man or woman; but this one was the King over the others.

"How handsome he is!" whispered Thumbelina to the swallow.

The little Prince was very much frightened at the swallow, for in comparison with one so tiny as himself he seemed a giant. But when he saw Thumbelina, he was delighted, for she was the most beautiful girl he had ever seen. So he took his golden crown from off his head and put it on hers, asking her name, and if she would be his wife, and then she would be Queen of all the flowers. Yes! he was a different kind of husband to the son of the toad and the mole with the black-velvet coat. She said "Yes" to the noble Prince. And out of each flower came a lady and gentleman, each so tiny and pretty that it was a pleasure to see them. Each brought Thumbelina a present, but the best of all was a beautiful pair of wings which were fastened on to her back, and now she too could fly from flower to flower. They all wished her joy, and the swallow sat above in his nest and sang the wedding march, and that he did as well as he could; but he was sad, because he was very fond of Thumbelina and did not want to be separated from her.

"You shall not be called Thumbelina!" said the spirit of the flower to her; "that is an ugly name, and you are much too pretty for that. We will call you May Blossom."

"Farewell, farewell!" said the little swallow with a heavy heart, and flew away to farther lands, far, far away, right back to Denmark. There he had a little nest above a window, where his wife lived, who can tell fairy-stories. "Tweet, tweet!" he sang to her. And that is the way we learnt the whole story.

Doll in the Grass

A tale from Norway

Here is the tale of a lady thumbling from Norway. The tale is usually told with a small animal as the maid who meets the prince rather than a miniature human. A frog is popular for this role. In those stories the animal becomes a real girl at the tale's end. In *this* story the tiny girl becomes a real girl and, of course, marries the prince.

This tale offers some vivid imagery, as well as a clever plot. The tiny girl's coach is a silver spoon, and her white horses are two white mice. Sibling rivalry again rears its ugly head as 12 brothers find themselves competing to win their father's favor by returning home with a fair bride.

Once on a time there was a King who had twelve sons. When they were grown big he told them they must go out into the world and win themselves wives, but these wives must each be able to spin, and weave, and sew a shirt in one day, else he wouldn't have them for daughters-in-law.

To each he gave a horse and a new suit of mail, and they went out into the world to look after their brides; but when they had gone a bit of the way, they said they wouldn't have Boots, their youngest brother, with them—he wasn't fit for anything.

Well, Boots had to stay behind, and he didn't know what to do or whither to turn; and so he grew so downcast, he got off his horse, and sat down in the tall grass to weep. But when he had sat a little while, one of the tufts in the grass began to stir and move, and out of it came a little white thing, and when it came nearer, Boots saw it was a charming little lassie, only such a tiny bit of a thing. So the lassie went up to him, and asked if he would come down below and see "Doll i' the Grass."

Yes, he'd be very happy; and so he went.

Now, when he got down, there sat Doll i' the Grass on a chair; she was so lovely and so smart, and she asked Boots whither he was going, and what was his business.

So he told her how there were twelve brothers of them, and how the King had given them horse and mail, and said they must each go out into the world and find them a wife who could spin, and weave, and sew a shirt in a day.

"But if you'll only say at once you'll be my wife, I'll not go a step farther," said Boots to Doll i' the Grass.

Well, she was willing enough, and so she made haste, and span, and wove, and sewed the shirt, but it was so tiny, tiny little. It wasn't longer than so ——— long.

So Boots set off home with it, but when he brought it out he was almost ashamed, it was so small. Still the King said he should have her, and so Boots set off, glad and happy to fetch his little sweetheart. So when he got to Doll i' the Grass, he wished to take her up before him on his horse; but she wouldn't have that, for she said she would sit and drive along in a silver spoon, and that she had two small white horses to draw her. So off they set, he on his horse and she on her silver spoon, and the two horses that drew her were two tiny white mice; but Boots always kept the other side of the road, he was so afraid lest he should ride over her, she was so little. So, when they had gone a bit of the way, they came to a great piece of water. Here Boots' horse got frightened, and shied across the road and upset the spoon, and Doll i' the Grass tumbled into the water. Then Boots got so sorrowful, because he didn't know how to get her out again; but in a little while up came a merman with her, and now she was as well and full grown as other men and women, and far lovelier than she had been before. So he took her up before him on his horse, and rode home.

When Boots got home all his brothers had come back each with his sweetheart, but these were all so ugly, and foul, and wicked, that they had done nothing but fight with one another on the way home, and on their heads they had a kind of hat that was daubed over with tar and soot, and so the rain had run down off the hats on to their faces, till they got far uglier and nastier than they had been before. When his brothers saw Boots and his sweetheart, they were all as jealous as jealous could be of her; but the King was so overjoyed with them both, that he drove all the others away, and so Boots held his wedding-feast with Doll i' the Grass, and after that they lived well and happily together a long time, and if they're not dead, why, they're alive still.

Notes to the Tales

Notes

Tale Types and Motifs

In these notes you will find references to tale types as used in *The Types of the Folktale* by Antti Aarne and Stith Thompson (Helsinki: Suomalainen Tiedeakatemia, 1973). They will look like this: Type 700 *Tom Thumb*. Each entire folktale is given a "type number" in the Aarne/Thompson classification scheme. A thumbling might appear in many different folktale types.

You will also find in these tale notes references to folktale *motifs*. These refer to the classification set out in the *Motif-Index of Folk-Literature* by Stith Thompson (Bloomington: Indiana University Press, 1966). They will look like this: F545.1.1 *Adventures of thumbling*. The motif-index indexes smaller parts of a tale, rather than assigning one number to the entire tale. Thus a thumbling tale might include motifs such as T543 *Birth from plant* or B641.0.1 *Marriage to person in animal form*. You will also see references to *The Storyteller's Sourcebook: A Subject, Title, and Motif-Index to Folklore Collections for Children* by Margaret Read MacDonald (Detroit: Neal-Schuman/Gale Research, 1982). This index is based on the indexing system in the Stith Thompson *Motif-Index to Folk-Literature*, but treats collections published for use with children.

Once you know the motif or type number of the folktale you want to study, you can look it up in other motif and type indexes. Several are available in academic libraries. If you go on a serious search for certain thumbling variants, those tools can help you. But all this is probably more than most users of this book will want to know.

Thumbling

This tale is taken from the 1884 translation by Margaret Hunt of *Grimm's Household Tales* by Jacob and Wilhelm Grimm (London: George Bell and Sons, 1884, pp. 153-58). The two volumes appeared in their first German edition in 1812 and 1814.

This is the basic tale of Type 700 *Tom Thumb*. The tale's description, as given in *The Types of the Folktale* is: "The tale includes: I *The Hero's birth*. A childless couple wish for a child, however small he may be; they have a boy the size of a thumb (F535.1). II *His Adventures* (F535.1.1) (a) He drives the wagon by sitting in the horse's ear; (b) he lets himself be sold and then runs away; (c) he is carried up the chimney by the steam of food; (d) he teases the tailor's wife; (e1) he helps thieves rob a treasure-house; (e2) he betrays the thieves by his cries; (f) he is swallowed by a cow (F911.3.1), makes an outcry (F913), and is rescued when the cow is slaughtered; (g1) he persuades the fox who has eaten him to go to his father's house and eat chickens, or (g2) the wolf to go to his father's pantry—he then calls for help and is rescued."

The Types of the Folktale by Antti Aarne and Stith Thompson lists many sources for this tale: German, Finnish, Swedish, Estonian, Livonian, Lithuanian, Norwegian, Danish, Icelandic, Irish, English, Basque, French, Spanish, Catalan, Dutch, Flemish, Austrian, Italian, Romanian, Hungarian, Czech, Slovenian, Serbocroatian, Polish, Russian, Greek, Turkish, Indian, French-American, Chilean, Dominican Republican, Puerto Rican, West Indian, and from the Cape Verde Islands.

Thumbling's Travels

Here is another tale taken from the 1884 translation by Margaret Hunt of *Grimms' Household Tales* by Jacob Grimm and Wilhelm Grimm (London: George Bell and Sons, 1884, pp. 174-77). This collection was first published in German in two volumes appearing in 1812 and 1814.

This is another German variant of Type 700. You will notice that certain elements of the "Thumbling" tale listed on page 137 are left out while others are elaborated or altered. Here the thumbling cooperates with the robbers and carries off a coin himself. And the fox who carries him home is rewarded.

The storyteller's voice is strong in this story, especially in the ending when the teller engages in dialogue with the listener.

Lipuniushka

"Lipuniushka" is reprinted from *Baba Yaga's Geese and Other Russian Stories*, translated and adapted by Bonnie Carey; illustrated by Guy Fleming (Bloomington: Indiana University Press, 1973, pp. 96-98). This tale is unusual in the thumbling's place of origin . . . in cotton being spun. Notice the other ethnic touches which identify this story as Russian, such as the blini (a type of pancake) and the barin (a socially prominent gentleman).

This is a variant of Type 700 (Motif F535.1.1).

Pouçot

This tale is taken from "Tom Thumb" in *Folktales of France*, edited by Geneviéve Massignon; translated by Jacqueline Hyland (Chicago: University of Chicago Press, 1968, p. 19). The tale was collected in 1960 from Mme. Bellion, age 65, from Bretignolles (Deux-Sevres).

Massignon tells us that the small hero of the French variants of Type 700 *Tom Thumb* might be called Pouçot, a term widely used in Nivernais, to differentiate them from the "Petit Poucet," which Perrault uses for his hero in Type 327 *The Children and the Ogre*.

Massignon notes that: "This tale is an example of this theme [Type 700], which is widespread in western France, where the adventures of Pouçot are well known and often interspersed with brief rhymed verses, smatterings of which quickly come to the minds of the old peasant women, even when they think they have forgotten the main content of the story."

Hasan, the Heroic Mouse-Child

This Turkish tale is a variant of Motif F535.1.1 (Type 700). Hasan takes lunch to his father, driving the donkey while riding in the saddlebag. His method of tricking the robbers by spying on them from a treetop is somewhat unusual. It is reminiscent of Motif K335.1.1.1 *Door falls on robbers from tree. They flee leaving money.*, a popular motif in other European tales.

Hasan's thrill at climbing the poplar tree so he can see the whole village is a delightful twist, and his transfer of the large golden coins, one at a time, pleases. Best of all is the tiny balcony built on the house roof at the story's end, "so that Hasan could watch all the people come and go." And Hasan's closing words add a useful moral to this tale. "Even a mouse-child can make himself tall enough to help his parents," says little Hasan.

"Hasan, the Heroic Mouse-Child" is reprinted from Barbara K. Walker's *A Treasury of Turkish Folktales for Children* (Hamden, CT: Linnet, 1988, pp. 8-10). The tales in this collection were retold by Barbara Walker from the over 3,000 Turkish tapes in the Archives of Turkish Oral Narrative at Texas Tech University. Barbara Walker and her husband, Harold Walker, have been researching in this area since 1961.

Loud Mouth Thummas

"Loud Mouth Thummas" draws inspiration from "Thumb-sized Thomas" in *The Golden Bird: Folk Tales from Slovenia* by Vladimir Kavcic; translated by Jan Dekker and Helen Lencek; illustrated by Mae Gerhard (Cleveland: World, 1969, pp. 87-92), and from other Eastern European variants. I chose this tale for retelling as a "tellable" tale because of its repeated episodes, its potential for lively banter between Thummas and the robbers, and the spunky nature of little Thummas. I call my tale "Loud Mouth Thummas" because that sums up his prime action in the tale. In this tale the thumbling plays a part in Motif K432 *Person being robbed deceives robbers and calls help*.

The Hazel-nut Child

This tale is reprinted from *The Yellow Fairy Book* by Andrew Lang (New York: Dover, 1966, pp. 222-24). Lang retold this tale from *Bukowniaer*, a collection of Bukovinian tales by Von Wliolocki. Bukovina is a region in the foothills of the Eastern Carpathian Mountains straddling the border of Romania and the Ukraine.

Here the thumbling drives horses by biting and pinching them. In this fashion, he drives the horse home with the horse thief still in the saddle! Later the thumbling flies to Africa aboard a stork and is so well received by the King there that he is given a diamond four times as big as himself.

Thumbikin

This tale is translated by George Webb Dasent from the collection of Peter Christen Asbjörnsen and Jörgen Moe. Their collections were published between 1841 and 1852 and were first translated into English in 1858 by George Webb Dasent. This particular tale is taken from *Popular Tales from the Norse* by Peter Christen Asbjörnsen and Jörgen Moe; translated by George Webb Dasent (Edinburgh, Scotland: David Douglas, 1888, pp. 372–73).

This unusual Norwegian variant begins with delightful play between Thumbikin and his mother as he hides repeatedly and jumps out calling "Pip, pip! Here I am!" This portion of the tale would make good fare for preschool storytelling. However the abrupt ending, in which poor Thumbikin falls into a puddle of melted butter and drowns, rather dampens the tale for use with contemporary audiences.

Piñoncito

This tale, translated by Margaret Read MacDonald, appears in *Cuentos Araucanos: La Gente de la Tierra* by Alicia Morel (Santiago, Chile: Editorial Andres Gello, 1982) and in *Revista de Historia y Geografia*, volume 26, by S. de Sauniers. The story was narrated by Rosario Concho of Linares and collected by S. de Sauniers in 1918.

The tale follows the thumbling pattern: small child helps parents, is swallowed by cow, etc. However, the roasting in the callampa plant and the lengthy stay in the bird's nest are unusual elements. Notice that the thumbling is described at one point as being half fairy, explaining his ability to understand the language of birds. Note also the magical element of the giant's bone.

Tom Thumb

This is the earliest Tom Thumb variant included in this collection. It was published in 1848 as *Popular Rhymes and Nursery Tales: A Sequel to the Nursery Rhymes of England* by James Orchard Halliwell-Phillipps (London: John Russell Smith, 1849, pp. 90-100). It is unclear what source Halliwell-Phillipps is drawing on for his tale, but he cites commentary from a 1711 publication by Dr. Wagstaffe titled *A Comment upon the History of Tom Thumb*.

Note how the basic thumbling tale has been incorporated into Arthurian mythology here. Tom is a resident of King Arthur's court. His small size is a misfortune cast when Merlin granted his parents' wish for a child, even a small one. The fairy queen attends his christening and Tom Thumb himself is called a "fairy boy."

The brief snatches of verse scattered through the tale are but hints of the fashion of the seventeenth and eighteenth centuries, when Tom's tale was often told entirely in verse. Halliwell-Phillipps apparently tired of the version he was retelling here and cuts it off abruptly, summarizing the ending in one paragraph.

Petit Poucet

"Petit Poucet" is reprinted from "Little Thumb" in Andrew Lang's *The Blue Fairy Book* (New York: Dover, 1965). The first English language translation of this tale appeared in 1729 as *Histories, or Tales of Past Times.* Little Thumb was called "Little Poucet" in that version, from the French "Petit Poucet." Later the English tale became known as "Hop O' My Thumb."

The French author Charles Perrault (1628-1703) set this story down along with "Sleeping Beauty," "Red Riding Hood," "Bluebeard," "Puss in Boots," "Cinderella," "Diamonds and Toads," and the forgotten tale "Riquet a la Houppe." His collection, called *Histoires Du Contes Du Temps Passé. Avec Des Moralitez* was published in Paris in January 1697. Perrault was at the time a retired civil servant and a member of the Academie Francaise. Though he had clearly learned these stories from the folk tradition, his publication of them and their ensuing popularity served to freeze these particular stories in a "correct" version henceforth. Though hundreds of variants of "Cinderella" have been collected, in our culture "Cinderella" usually recalls the version set down by Charles Perrault.

This thumbling is Type 327 *The Children and the Ogre.* The French Petit Poucet has a quite different adventure than the English Tom Thumb. Charles Perrault used a thumbling as the main character in the saga of the small hero who defeats an ogre to rescue siblings. This tale turns on the cleverness of its main motif K1611. *Substituted caps cause ogre to kill his own children. The hero and heroine change places in bed with the ogre's children and put on them their caps so the ogre is deceived.* In English translation this tale is known as "Hop 'O My Thumb." Compare "Hop 'O My Thumb" with "Molly Whuppie" in Joseph Jacobs' *English Folk and Fairy Tales* (New York: Putnam, n.d., pp. 130-35) and "Mutsmag" in *Grandfather Tales* by Richard Chase (Boston: Houghton Mifflin, 1948, pp. 45-52). MacDonald's *Storyteller's Sourcebook* includes 12 variants of Motif K1611, from 10 cultures.

Fereyel and Debbo Engal the Witch

"Fereyel and Debbo Engal the Witch" is reprinted from *African Myths and Legends,* retold by Kathleen Arnott and illustrated by Joan Kiddell-Monroe (New York: Henry Z. Walck, Inc., 1962, pp. 200-11). Arnott does not indicate the ethnic origin of the tale and I have been unable to discover which culture tells this story. I decided to include it anyway because it is a good example of the use of a thumbling in Motif K1611.

Although we don't know from which part of Africa this tale came, the tale itself gives us several clues about the setting. It might be fun to let your listeners/readers look for clues in the story that give information about the area where the tale took place. Examples: The brothers went into the bush. They collected logs. They found wild plum trees. They used calabashes to carry the fruit. They rode donkeys. They believed that a python could appear on the path. A linguist could probably identify the tale's origin from the characters' unusual names . . . Fereyel and Debbo Engal.

Digit the Midget

"Digit the Midget" is reprinted from *The Lion's Whiskers: Tales of High Africa* by Russell Davis and Brent Ashabranner; illustrated by James Teason (Boston: Little, Brown, and Co., 1959, pp. 53-61).

Ashabranner writes: "Amhara children and grown-ups enjoy the adventures of a clever midget called Sinzero. The name Sinzero comes from the Amharic word *sinzer,* the measure of the distance from the tip of the thumb to the tip of the longest finger. We have translated the name Sinzero to Digit in our story, although the actual translation of the word would be 'span.' The span is still used as a measure of length in Ethiopia, and it was once used in England and America.

Actually there are two midgets in Ethiopian storyland. The other one's name is Aure Tat, from the word for 'thumb.' Both of the Ethiopian midgets appear in hundreds of stories. In one series of stories, Digit became a house burglar. He entered the house by riding underneath a cat."

The thumbling in this tale is a trickster. He is rejected by his seven older brothers but gets even over and over. Digit makes a drum from the bladder of a stolen bull and sings that his brothers stole it. Then the tale turns to a combination of Type 1539 *Cleverness and Gullibility—The youth sells pseudo-magic objects and animals* and Type 1535 *The Rich and Poor Peasant*. Digit convinces his brothers to burn down their houses to ashes (K941.2 *Dupe burns house because trickster reports high price paid for ashes.*). He passes off a magic, gold-producing basket to a stranger and rides away on the stranger's horse (K110 *Sale of pseudo-magic objects.*). He tells each of his seven brothers that his horse came from a different place, then ties their legs together while they sleep and watches them trip each other up in the morning. This is an unusual ending as in most variants of Type 1535 the trickster says he got his horse (sheep) from the bottom of the river and his brothers dive in and never return.

Boy-Man

This tale is reprinted from *Indian Fairy Tales as Told by Little Children of the Wigwam* by Mary Hazelton Wade (Great Neck, NY: Core Collection, reprinted 1979; original publication, 1906, pp. 101-09). The tale includes traditional thumbling acts such as the swallowed by fish motif: F912 *Victim kills swallower from within.*

The killing of the large men as they peer, one by one, into the hole in his door stone is similar to the killing of the robbers as they enter one by one (Motif K912) in "Three Inch." However the brother-sister relationship and the unusual gathering of fireflies at the tale's end are specific to this Native American tale. Stories of small brothers who protect their sisters appear in several Native American collections. Compare this tale with "The Mouse and the Sun" in *Canadian Wonder Tales* by Cyrus MacMillan (London: Bodley Head, 1974, pp. 30-33).

The Snail *Choja*

"The Snail *Choja*" is reprinted from *Folktales of Japan* by Keigo Seki; translated by Robert J. Adams with a foreword by Richard M. Dorson (Chicago: University of Chicago Press, 1963, pp. 40-43). The tale was collected in Tono-mura, Kamihei-gun, Iwate-ken from Kinzo Ogasawara.

"The Snail *Choja*" is not a thumbling story. Instead it is one of the many tales of supernatural animal brides or bridegrooms. B641.0.1 *Marriage to person in animal form*. "The Frog Prince" is another of this type tale with which many are familiar. I wanted to include one such tale because it is interesting to compare the problems of the diminutive-sized creatures in these "animal husband" tales with those of Tom Thumb. Note one important difference in these tales though: the "animal husband" eventually regains his true size. Tom Thumb remains a thumbling.

Notice the strong spiritual basis of this Japanese variant. The snail child is the gift of a water deity. He is kept on the home altar, and throughout his life the parents pray to the water deity and attribute all to that spirit's benevolence. It is because of the young bride's worship at the shrine of Yakushi-*sama* that the snail child finally attains a human form. The young bride's sad song as she wanders in the muddy rice fields looking for her lost snail husband provides an unusual and striking element in this folktale.

Seki notes that in Japan, where to be childless is considered extremely unfortunate, a couple's desire for a child of any kind, even a snail child, would be accepted as natural by the hearers of the tale. Brides returned to visit their parents a month or more after marriage. At that time they also reported their marriage to the graves of their ancestors. This visit completed the marriage formalities.

The Diminutive Flute Player

"The Diminutive Flute Player" is reprinted from *Burmese Folktales* by Maung Htin Aung (New Delhi: Oxford University Press, 1948, pp.

97-100). While it seems logical to classify the tale with Type 700 there are several quite different elements here. In this story the thumbling plays a part in Motif S143 *Children abandoned in woods*. He is abandoned repeatedly by his parents in the woods but returns, riding first a crocodile and then a tiger.

Maung Htin Aung mentions that the number four is important in Burmese folktales. A hero has four followers, four magical weapons, four adventures. The fourth brother is luckiest and most handsome.

Three Inch

"Three Inch" was inspired by *Toontoony Pie and Other Tales from Pakistan* by Ashraf Siddiqui and Marilyn Lerch (Cleveland, OH; New York: The World Publishing Company, 1961, pp. 91-97). This amazing story starts with a thumbling and throws in every sort of trickster motif, a king who demands a reward, and a princess who needs to be healed! A helpful frog and a miniature blacksmith add to the curiosity. Thumbling ties the blacksmith's beard (F451.6.1), frees the frog's wife and is rewarded with magic curing liquid (D2161.3.1), and beheads eight robbers as they enter one by one (K912. *Robbers' [giants'] heads cut off one by one as they enter house*. Type 304). The tale ends with the thumbling marrying the princess and gaining acceptance despite his small stature.

In this tale the thumbling's physical appearance caused him to be rejected. Notice that in Maung Htin Aung's introduction to "Master Thumb" (included in the tale notes for "Little Thumb Conquers the Sun") the Burmese thumbling also suffers from being mocked.

For a more elaborate version of this tale see *The Cucumber Stem* by Betsy Bang; illustrated by Tony Chen (New York: Greenwillow, 1980). Bang drew her version from a Bengali tale. In her version "Little Finger" rides a black cat to the robbers' palace, where the cat eats everything in sight. Then Little Finger releases a gourd full of bees to rout the robbers. At the tale's end an old woman gives him a cucumber and warns him to eat it stem and all. He obeys and is turned into a real man. Chen's illustrations are delightful and Bang's retelling is excellent. Highly recommended for sharing as a picture book, despite its small "I-Can-Read" format.

Little Shell

"Little Shell" was inspired by *Once in the First Times: Folk Tales from the Philippines* by Elizabeth Hough Sechrist (Philadelphia, PA: Macrae Smith Company, 1969, pp. 93-97) and by thumbling tales in *Philippine Folk Literature: The Folktales*, compiled and edited by Damiana L. Eugenio (Quezon City, Philippines: U.P. Folklorists, Inc., in cooperation with the Philippine National Science Society, 1989, pp. 145-46, 192-200.) This is a Visayan folktale, told much like other thumbling tales until Little Shell decides to send his mother to ask for the hand of the headman's daughter. The girl says "Yes," bringing the tale to an abrupt and happy ending.

Issun Boshi

"Issun Boshi" is based on "Little One Inch" in *Folktales of Japan* edited by Keigo Seki; translated by Robert J. Adams with a foreword by Richard M. Dorson (Chicago: University of Chicago Press, 1963, pp. 90-92); *Issun Boshi, the Inchling* by Momoko Ishii (New York: Walker, 1965); "Issun Boshi, the One-Inch Lad" in Yoshiko Uchida's *Dancing Kettle* (New York: Harcourt, Brace, 1949); and other children's retellings.

The retelling presented in this book is designed for use in audience participation storytelling and is recommended for preschool and primary children. Let them join with you on repeated phrases such as "still . . . one inch tall." Encourage them to row with Issun Boshi as he makes his way downstream. It works well for the children to row awhile, then rest on their oars and drift, then row some more. If you are comfortable with improvisation, let the children suggest games that Issun Boshi and the princess played together, then elaborate on how he employed his tiny size for gain in those games.

This thumbling story is unusual in that Issun Boshi turns into a normal-sized boy at the story's end and marries the princess. Compare this story to other Japanese tales such as "Momotaro" (in *The Dancing Kettle* by Yoshiko Uchida) and "The Snail Choja" (see p. 77). Does it seem more influenced by *those* stories or by the European Tom Thumb tradition? Students might want to make a list of the characteristics in this story that make it distinctly Japanese.

Seki notes that his version was collected in Tokorozawa-mura, Iruma-gun, Saitama-ken, from the maid of collector Mitsue Hitabayashi.

Little Thumb Conquers the Sun

"Little Thumb Conquers the Sun" is a retelling based on "Master Thumb" in *Burmese Folk-Tales* by Maung Htin Aung (New Delhi: Oxford University Press, 1948, pp. 93-97). To make this story easy to learn and tell, I pared Maung Htin Aung's version down a bit, leaving out some description, repeating the same dialogue with each helper met, and elaborating that dialogue. I also expanded the ogre scene and the ending, adding dialogue and parallel refrains for a pleasing, "tellable" flow. In order to make the story work better for younger audiences, I dropped the interesting opening of Maung Htin Aung's story and changed the thumbling's motivation slightly. Here is the actual opening to the Burmese tale:

Once a poor woman who was with child was trying to dry some paddy. But the moment she put out her basket of paddy the Sun disappeared, and the moment she took in her basket thinking it was going to rain, the Sun shone bright and clear again. This was repeated so many times that the woman lost her temper and abused the Sun roundly. The Sun in return laid upon her a curse, with the result that when her son was born later he was no bigger than a man's thumb. The child was given the name of Master Thumb.

Master Thumb felt very unhappy because other children made fun of his small stature, and when he attained the ripe age of sixteen years he demanded of his mother the true reason of his being no bigger than a thumb. When he learnt that the Sun's curse was the cause, he said, "Mother, make me a big cake tomorrow, as I am going in search of the Sun to fight him."

While my straight-to-the-story retelling works well for preschool and primary listeners, older students attempting to analyze these Tom Thumb variants should also hear this unusual introduction to the actual Burmese tale.

Maung Htin Aung tells us that his is an Upper Burma version of this tale. He describes a Lower Burma version in which the companions are Slab of Rock, Village Rest House, Tiger, and Cat. The ogre is omitted. Instead the extended fight takes place with the Sun itself. The Sun also has followers, who engage in battle with Master Thumb's companions.

The Sun said to his follower the Thunderbolt, "Go and kill Master Thumb." The Thunderbolt rushed towards Master Thumb, but the Slab of Rock jumped out of the stomach, and protected his little master. The Sun then said to his follower the Rain, "Go and kill Master Thumb." The Rain rushed towards Master Thumb, but the Village Rest House jumped out of the stomach and protected his little master. The Sun then said to his follower the Bull, "Go and kill Master Thumb." The Bull rushed towards Master Thumb but the Tiger jumped out of the stomach and, by eating up the Bull, protected his little master. The Sun then said to his follower the cock, "Go and kill Master Thumb." The Cock rushed towards Master Thumb, but the Cat jumped out of the stomach, and saved his little master by eating up the cock. The Sun now had no followers left, and he himself rushed towards Master Thumb. In the ensuing duel, the Sun was defeated, and had to ask for pardon from Master Thumb. Master Thumb, being a magnanimous young hero, pardoned the Sun, after making him promise that he would not lay curses on human beings again.

In this story the thumbling plays a role in Motif Z52 *Bird avenges mate. Arms self and proclaims war with King. Collects cat, ants, stick, and river (all jump into his ear)....* You might want to compare this story to "Drakestail" in *Favorite Fairy Tales Told in France* by Virginia Haviland

(Boston: Little, Brown, 1959, pp. 76-91) and to "Half Chick" in Ruth Sawyer's *Picture Tales from Spain* (New York: Lippincott, 1936, pp. 97-110). See Motif Z52 in *The Storyteller's Sourcebook* by Margaret Read MacDonald (Neal-Schuman/Gale Research, 1982) for several variants of this tale in which a small hero swallows companions who later emerge to assist. "Master Thumb" (in the Upper Burma variant) also uses Motif K1161 *Animals hidden in various parts of a house attack owner with their characteristic powers and kill him when he enters.*

Compare this story with the Brothers Grimm tale "The Bremen Town Musicians," to be found in Veronica Hutchinson's *Chimney Corner Fairy Tales* (New York: Minton Balch, 1926, pp. 127-34), in Richard Chase's *Jack Tales* (Boston: Houghton Mifflin, 1946, pp. 40-46), and in most collections of the fairy tales of the Brothers Grimm. A Venezuelan Juan Bobo tale using this motif is included in *King of the Mountains* by Moritz Jagendorf and Ralph Steel Boggs (New York: Vanguard, 1960, pp. 269-73). See *The Storyteller's Sourcebook* by Margaret Read MacDonald (Neal-Schuman/Gale Research, 1982) for over 22 variants of Motif K1161, from 22 different countries.

Thumbling the Giant

This tale appeared as "The Young Giant" in *Household Tales* by Jacob and Wilhelm Grimm; it was translated and edited by Margaret Hunt (London: George Bell and Sons, 1884, pp.174-77)

In this tale Thumbling has been cast as hero in Type 650A *Strong John.* Included are Motif F613.1 *Strong man's labor contest: blow at end of years. Blow sends his master to sky;* F615.3.1.1 *Strong hero asks that chickens stop scratching. When his master throws millstones on him he complains that chickens are scratching dirt on him;* F615.3 *Strong hero overawes master;* H1411 *Fear test: staying in a haunted house;* F615.3.1 *Strong man attacked with millstone puts it on as a collar;* and F615.1 *Strong man sent to Devil's mill.*

However, unlike other Strong John tales, this one begins with the birth of a thumbling who is nurtured by a giant until he attains his huge stature (F611.2.5 *Strong hero suckled by giant;* also D55.1.3 *Pygmy turns into a giant*).

Tough Little Niraidak

The thumbling in this Evenk tale from Siberia bears resemblance to our other thumblings only in size and in spunky attitude. Niraidak rides a magic deer that can change to a fire-breathing boar. He challenges a giant, carries off a beautiful maiden, and is undaunted by his inability to impress either. This is a delightfully different invention on the theme of the very tiny individual.

For a more elaborate telling of this story see "Niraidak: An Evenk Fairy Tale" in *Northern Lights: Fairy Tales of the Peoples of the North* by E. Pomerantseva; retold by Irina Zheleznova (Moscow: Progress Publishers, 1976, pp. 165-67).

Thumbelina

Hans Christian Andersen's "Tommelise" was first published in Copenhagen in 1836. It was transcribed into English in 1846, but it wasn't until an 1864 translation appeared that the name "Thumbelina" became attached to our heroine. This translation is taken from Andrew Lang's *Yellow Fairy Book* (New York: Dover, 1966, pp. 283-96).

Andersen, like the sparrow, had been nursed by a wee maid at one time in his life. There is speculation that the story may have been a tribute to Henriette Wulff, the small, hunchbacked daughter of one of Andersen's friends. Henriette had cared for Andersen while he was ill.

In this story Andersen takes a simple folktale theme—the small child adrift in a huge world full of dangers—and embroiders it with his remarkable imagination. Though Thumbelina has some adventures that mirror Tom Thumb's, this piece is a literary fantasy, far removed from its folktale origins.

Doll in the Grass

"Doll in the Grass" appears in *Norwegian Folk and Fairy Tales* by Peter Asbjörnsen and Jörgen Moe. The first of these tales was published in 1841. The annotated edition published in 1851 was translated into English by George Webb Dasent and published in 1858. Our version is taken from *Popular Tales from the Norse* by Peter Christen Asbjörnsen and Jörgen Moe (Edinburgh: David Douglas, 1888, pp. 374–76).

This tale is a variant of B641.0.1 *The Mouse (Cat, Frog, etc.) as bride* (Type 402). MacDonald's *Storyteller's Sourcebook* lists variant tales from Italy, Switzerland, the Philippines, Germany, the Ukraine, Russia, Portugal, Yugoslavia, France, Finland, Sweden, Denmark, India, Egypt, and Poland.

In other versions the maid is a frog, mouse, monkey, cat, white fox, tortoise, and in one case a cow. In our Norwegian version the maid is a miniature *girl*, rather than an animal. A delightful Yugoslavian version with the maid as a *frog* is "The Little Singing Frog" in *The Laughing Prince* by Parker Fillmore (New York: Harcourt, Brace & World, 1961, pp. 163-70).

For an airy Vietnamese variation on this tale see "Little Finger of the Watermelon Patch" in *The Brocaded Slipper and Other Vietnamese Tales* by Lynette Dyer Vuong (New York: Lippincott, 1982, pp. 27-43). In this version Little Finger is a fairy under a spell. The tale includes charming imagery of Little Finger at play in the watermelon patch.

Essays,
Activities, and
Resources

Early Print Versions of Tom Thumb

Tom Thumb is an especially interesting tale to examine because early printings of the story still exist. Earliest of these is a 40-page booklet printed in 1621. The booklet's cover reads *The History of Tom Thumbe, the Little, for his small stature surnamed, King Arthurs Dwarfe: Whose Life and adventures containe many strange and wonderfull accidents, published for the delight of merry Time-spenders.* Imprinted at London for Tho Langley, 1621. The folktales from which this story was created must have been ancient even at this time. The author, who signs himself "R.J." and is believed to be Richard Johnson (1573-1659?), tells us:

> The ancient Tales of Tom Thumbe in the olde time, have been the onely revivers of drozy age at midnight; old and young have with his Tales chim'd Mattens till the Cocks crow in the morning; Batchelors and Maides with his Tales have compassed the Christmas fire-blocke, till the Curfew Bell rings candle out; the old Shepheard and the young Plow boy after their dayes labour, have carold out a Tale of Tom Thumbe to make them merry with: and who but little Tom, hath made long night seem short, & heavy toyles easie?

As early as 1584 the censors were trying to protect children from such frightening children's stories. Reginald Scot, in his *Discoverie of Witchcraft*, warned of stories of "bull-beggers, spirits, witches, urchens, elves, hags, fairies, satyrs, pans, faunes, sylens, kit with the canstick, tritons, centaures, dwarfes, giants, imps" with which servant maids had so affrighted people in their childhood "that we are afraid of our owne shadows." He lumps Tom Thumbe in with this lot.

The novelty of this small creature seems to have caught the imagination of folks from the fifteenth through the nineteenth centuries. His adventures were reprinted again and again. Each author lent his own twist to Tom's plot. The 1621 version finds Tom a popular member of the court of King Arthur, receiving magic gifts from a fairy godmother. Later versions, reverting to more common folktale motifs, merely move tiny Tom from one oversized disaster to another . . . he is swallowed by a cow, meets a giant, is lost in a pudding, etc.

Many of Tom's early versions break frequently into rhyme and several popular versions were presented entirely in verse. One of these was *Tom Thumbe, His Life and Death: Wherein is declared many Maruailous Acts of Manhood, full of wonder, and strange merriments: Which little Knight lived in King Arthurs time, and famours in the Court of Great-Brittaine* (London. Printed for John Wright, 1630).

By the 1700s Tom Thumb's tale was being used to parody literary criticism. William Wagstaff, in 1711, wrote *A Comment upon the History of Tom Thumb* in a parody of Addison's comments on the ballad "Chevy Chase." In his introduction he speaks, with tongue only slightly in cheek, of the value of Tom Thumb:

> It was my good fortune, some time ago, to have the library of a schoolboy committed to my charge, where, among other undiscovered valuable authors, I pitched upon Tom Thumb and Tom Hickathrift, authors indeed more proper to adorn the shelves of Bodley or the Vatican, than to be confined to the retirement and obscurity of a private study. I have perused the first of these with an infinite pleasure, and a more than ordinary application, and have made some observations on it, which may not, I hope, prove unacceptable to the public, and however it may have been ridiculed and looked upon as an entertainment only for children and those of younger years, may be found perhaps a performance not unworthy the perusal of the judicious, and the

model superior to either of those incomparable poems of Chevy Chase or the Children in the Wood. The design was undoubtedly to recommend virtue, and to show that however any one may labour under the disadvantages of stature and deformity, or the meanness of parentage yet if his mind and actions are above the ordinary level, those very disadvantages that seem to depress him add a lustre to his character.

In 1730 the Haymarket Theatre produced *Tom Thumb, A Tragedy.* The play was a parody for adults, imitating the take-themselves-too-seriously dramas and literature of the day. The play is a broad comedy. Tom Thumb is awarded the King's daughter, Huncamunca, in return for slaying the giants, but the Queen herself is in love with Tom Thumb. After much fast-paced intrigue the play ends with Tom being swallowed by a cow on the street. But his ghost returns and the play ends in a frenzy of slaying that must have left the audience roaring with laughter. This sample will give you a taste of the comedy.

Noodle reports:

When on a sudden through the Streets there
    came
A Cow of larger than the usual Size,
And in a moment, guess, oh! guess the rest,
And in a moment swallow'd up Tom Thumb.
King: Horrible indeed!
Lord Grizzel: Swallow'd she him alive?
Noodle: Alive, alive, Lord Grizzel,
so the Boys of Fishmongers do swallow Gudgeons down.
Lord Grizzel: Curse on the Cow that took my
    Vengeance from me. (Grizzel was hoping to
    slay Tom Thumb himself.)
King: Shut up again the Prisions, bid my Treasurer
not give three Farthings out—hang all the Culprits,
guilty or not—not matter—ravish Virgins,
Go bid the School-masters whip all their Boys,
Let Lawyers, Parsons and Physicians loose,
To Rob, impose on, and to kill the World.
The Ghost of Tom Thumb rises.

Ghost: Tom Thumb I am—but am not eke alive.
My Body's in the Cow, my Ghost is here.
Grizzel: Thanks, O ye Stars, my Vengeance is
    restor'd,
Nor shalt thou fly me—for I'll kill the Ghost.
Kills the Ghost.
Huncamunca: O barbarous Deed—I will revenge
    him so.
Kills Grizzel.
Doodle: Ha! Grizzel kill'd—then Murtheress beware.
Kills Huncamunca.
Queen: O wretch—have at thee.
Kills Doodle.
Noodle: And have at thee too.
Kills Queen.
Cleora (lady): Thou'st kill'd the Queen.
Kills Noodle.
Mustacha (lady): And thou hast kill'd my Lover.
Kills Cleora.
King: Ha! Murtheress vile, take that.
Kills Mustacha.
And take thou this!
Kills himself and falls.
So when the Child whom Nurse from Mischief
    guards,
Sends Jack for Mustard with a Pack of Cards,
Kings, Queens and Knaves, throw one another
    down,
Till the whole Pack lies scatter'd and o-erthrown;
So all our Pack upon the Floor is cast,
And all I boast is, that I fall the last.
Dies.
FINIS.

Two early versions of this play are printed in *The Tragedy of Tragedies or the Life and Death of Tom Thumb the Great with the annotations of H. Scriblerus Secundus* by Henry Fielding: edited by James T. Hillhouse (New Haven, CT: Yale University Press, 1918). For comment on early versions of thumbling tales along with interesting reproductions of early book illustrations see "The History of Tom Thumb," "Hop O' My Thumb," and "Thumbelina" in *The Classic Fairy Tales* by Iona and Peter Opie (London: Oxford University Press, 1974).

Mundig

Dear Reader:

You should note that poor Mundig has been banished to the Appendix by my editor for Mundig's wanton behavior. Such is the fate of all thumblings who go *beyond* socially acceptable limits.

—*The Author.*

Mundig
A tale from Armenia

Here is a very strange thumbling tale. Its gruesome touches make it unsuitable for sharing with groups. But it is interesting to consider as yet another variant thumbling story. Tales of little tricksters who eat the children of their enemies are not unusual in folk literature.

In this story the thumbling is born from a pea (along with hundreds of other tiny children). The overwhelmed mother, in an attempt to rid herself of the children, puts them in a hot oven. One of them, Mundig, survives and goes on to cause all sorts of trouble before disappearing, never to be heard from again.

―――――――――

Once upon a time in a peaceful village in Armenia there lived an old couple. Though these people very much wanted to have children, their wish had not been granted.

One day the woman was sitting outside her home when a dervish went by. "I wonder if this dervish can tell me what I must do to have children," the woman said to herself. "Dervish *Aga* [lord], won't you come here?" she asked him.

"What is it you want, woman?" the dervish said, coming close.

"Dervish *Aga*, I don't have a child, and I want one very much. What can I do?"

The dervish did not answer but began writing and writing and finally turned to her: "If you get a handful of *sissair* [chickpeas] and sit on it, you will have a child."

The woman was very happy for now at last she would have a child, her very own. She took a handful of *sissair* and did as the dervish had said. And sure enough! a whole bunch of babies, about as big as your thumb, were scattered all through the room! "Oh, what shall I do with all these little things?" the poor woman said, hitting her hands on her knees, pulling her hair and crying. "What shall I do with all these tiny things?"

In the midst of all this she remembered suddenly that she had to prepare her husband's lunch. So she hurriedly heated the oven and started to bake the bread. "I know what to do! I'll put all these little babies in the oven right now and get rid of them!"

After she had baked the bread, she took all the babies and put them into the hot oven. Of course, they all died immediately. "Oh, dear me, what have I done? I should have saved at least one of them to take lunch to his father!" the woman exclaimed.

But, contrary to what she thought, not all the babies had died: one had slipped through her fingers and escaped. When the baby heard his mother's words, he called out, "Mama, I'm here."

"Where are you, my child?" the mother asked.

"I'm up here," the baby said as he climbed up the wall.

"Come down, Mundig [Tiny], and take your father's lunch to him," the mother said. So the child became known as Mundig.

The mother prepared the lunch and tied it to Mundig's back. But needless to say, the lunch was bigger than the little boy. "You wait here, Mundig, while I go and get the donkey out," his mother said. She got the donkey out and seated Mundig right on his back. But what do you think Mundig did? He crawled from the donkey's back and hopped right into the donkey's ear! Oh! he liked it there.

Mundig and the donkey reached a field where there was a man plowing. "That must be my father," Mundig said to himself. "Father, father, come and get your lunch," Mundig called out from the donkey's ear.

The father looked up and saw the donkey without a rider. "When did this donkey of ours begin speaking and calling me father? I imagined it, no doubt," the man said to himself and returned to his plowing.

But no sooner had he resumed his work than he heard the voice saying, "Father, father, come and get your lunch."

"This is very strange," the man said. "I wonder who this is for I surely can't see anyone on that donkey. Child, child, where are you?" the father called out.

"I am in the donkey's ear," Mundig said.

The father took his baby and his lunch out of the donkey's ear. "What is your name?" he asked.

"My name is Mundig. Let me plow while you eat, father."

"No, my son, you will fall under the oxen's manure." But when the boy continued to beg, the father said, "All right, Mundig, but be careful. Don't walk directly behind the oxen."

Mundig was very happy. He started to plow a while, but he was not careful and soon fell under the oxen's manure. "Father, father, come help me! I'm under the oxen's manure," Mundig yelled.

"Didn't I tell you to be careful?" his father said, pulling the tiny boy out. "Oh, Mundig, you are so dirty! Come, I'll take you to the brook and wash you."

Mundig knew what it meant not to listen to his father, so he went along quietly. Soon they reached the brook, and his father began bathing him. "Mundig, don't look up," he said.

"Why, father?"

"There is an apple tree above us."

Mundig glanced upward and saw a beautiful tree heavy with juicy ripe apples. "Oh, if I could only get up there," Mundig said to himself. Presently, when Mundig's father had loosened his hold on him, Mundig jumped right up into the apple tree! It happened so quickly that the father could not stop him. "These apples are so good!" Mundig said, eating one apple after another.

"Mundig, come down," his father ordered.

"I'm going to eat these apples."

"Mundig, come down or you'll fall," his father repeated. But when Mundig did not answer him, he said, "All right then, if you aren't coming down, at least give me an apple."

Now Mundig knew what his father meant to do. He knew that if he should bend over to give the apple to his father, he would be caught and forced to come down. So instead of handing down the apple as he should have done, he threw it down.

"That Mundig is really a smart boy," his father said under his breath. "Come, Mundig, give me another apple," he called out.

And again, Mundig threw the apple down.

"Mundig, come down, come down," the father asked. But when Mundig continued to sit in the tree and eat apples, the father left him and returned to his plowing. When Mundig had eaten all the apples he wanted, he began to think of what to do next. "Where shall I go? Home? No! I know what: I'll try to find my aunt's house." So off he went, running and playing, to find his aunt's house.

However, his father had seen him running away. "I'd better go home and tell my wife about it," he said and started for home. "Wife, our son has run away," he told her.

"Our little Mundig? Oh, what shall we do!" his wife said, crying and hitting her hands on her knees. Mundig's father went back to the field, and his mother sat at home crying.

Mundig, meanwhile, found his aunt's house. "Aunty, I am here," he called.

"Mundig, is that you? Come in," she said. She had heard of him but had not yet seen him.

So Mundig went inside the house.

"Oh, Mundig, does your mother know that you are here?" his aunt asked. When Mundig avoided answering her, she said, "All right, Mundig, you stay here while I go and tell your mother not to worry."

Mundig noticed that his aunt was preparing supper. "I wonder what she is making," Mundig said, lifting the cover of the pan. And what a delicious treat did he see: his favorite food—lamb, cut into small pieces and roasted until tender and tasty. "Let me just taste a piece," Mundig said to himself, taking first one piece, then a second, then a third, until finally the very last piece of meat was gone.

"What shall I do now? I've eaten all the meat, and if my aunt finds out, she'll hit me!" Mundig said to himself. He looked around and saw his baby cousin in her cradle. "I know what to do!" he said. "I'll put my cousin in the pan, and they will never know the difference."

So he took his little cousin, put her in the pan and put the pan on the stove. Just as he finished doing this, he heard footsteps coming near. "Oh, I'll have to hide somewhere, or my aunt will hit me for eating all the meat," Mundig said. He looked around and noticed that there was nowhere he could hide. "Oh, the ceiling! She can never get me there!" Mundig said, quickly scaling the wall and getting up to the ceiling.

His aunt and mother walked into the house. They looked around for Mundig but could not find him. "Mundig, where are you, Mundig?" they called. But no Mundig was to be found. "Well, sister, come let's eat something first and then go out to look for him," the aunt said.

They poured some of the contents of the pan into two dishes and sat down to eat. The aunt put her spoon in and drew out an earring. "What is my baby's earring doing here?" she asked. "Where is my baby?" she cried, running to the cradle. Of course, she could not find the baby in the cradle. "Oh, that Mundig! He ate the meat and put his cousin in the pan. What shall I do? My beautiful baby!"

In this excitement Mundig escaped through the window.

Both mother and aunt ran outside looking for Mundig. "If I catch him, I'll do the same thing to him that he did to my baby," the aunt said, weeping.

Mundig walked and walked until he met a man playing a fiddle. Mundig took the fiddle away from the man, and the man was so frightened that he ran away. Mundig took the fiddle and started to sing:

"Oof, my fiddle, oof my fiddle,
My mother wanted a baby and couldn't have one.
She asked a passing dervish what she could do;
He told her to sit on a handful of *sissair*,
She did, and a lot of small babies were born.

"'What shall I do with all these tiny babies?'
    my mother asked herself;
She put them all in the oven and killed them,
    but I escaped.

'Oh, what did I do, what did I do!' my mother said.
'I didn't even leave one so that he could carry his father's lunch.'
I was on the wall and said, 'Mother, I'm here'.
'Where are you, son?' she asked.
'Right here on the wall,' I said.

"'Come down, Mundig, and take your father's lunch,' she said.
She tied the lunch to my back and put me on the donkey's back.
I slipped from the donkey's back into his ear.
I took my father's lunch.
I wanted to plow, but my father wouldn't let me.

"Finally I plowed, but I fell under the oxen's manure.
My father picked me out and took me to the brook to wash me.
There was a big apple tree right above us, and when my father loosened his grip on me,
I jumped up the apple tree and began eating.
'Come down, Mundig, come down,' my father said.
'No, I won't come down,' I said.
'Come, Mundig, or you'll fall,' my father said.
'No, I won't come down,' I said.

"'All right, then, give me an apple,' my father said.
I was too smart to give him an apple so I threw him one.
Finally, my father went home and told my mother that I had run away.
I went to my aunt's house.
My aunt went to tell my mother not to worry about me.
When she was away, I ate all the supper.

"I put my little cousin in the pan and put it on the stove.
My aunt and mother came home and couldn't find me.
I was watching from the ceiling.

They sat down to eat a little before looking for
me.
My aunt put her spoon in the meat and found
an earring.
'Whose earring is this?' she asked.
She ran to her baby's cradle and found her
baby missing.
'Mundig ate all the supper and put my little
baby in the pan instead!' my aunt cried.
They went out to find me, but I escaped.

"I walked and walked and saw a man playing
a fiddle.
I took his fiddle away from him, and he was
frightened and ran away.
Now I'm playing and singing.
Oof, my fiddle, I'm playing and singing."

Just then Mundig saw his mother and aunt
coming toward him. He took his fiddle and ran
away again. He walked and walked until he saw
three musicians playing different instruments. "I
think I'll join these men," Mundig said, playing
on his fiddle. He jumped from one musician's lap
to another's, playing on his fiddle all the while.

Mundig looked down the road and again saw
his mother and aunt approaching. Holding tightly
to his fiddle, he ran and ran and jumped in the
river.

And no one has ever seen Mundig since.

A Note About Mundig

This tale is reprinted from *100 Armenian Tales and
Their Folkloristic Relevance*, collected and edited by
Susie Hoogasian-Villa (Detroit, MI: Wayne State University, 1966, pp 235-40). The tale was told by Mrs.
Mariam Serabian.

This story contains the unusual motif of a
thumbling being born from a pea (T543 *Birth from
plant*). In fact hundreds of children are born from the
peas, but only one survives. Mundig's atrocious behavior in eating up his aunt's stew and replacing the
meat with her baby is too horrible for contemporary
children, but was a fairly common motif in folktales.
This theme is also common in the folklore of children,
and is said by psychologists to be cathartic in dealing
with their own jealousy of new, demanding siblings.

Mundig's musical recap of the entire tale at the
end is also an unusual touch. The tune for his song was
not included in Hoogasian-Villa's text.

A Whole Language Curriculum for Tom Thumb

This book can be used as a base collection for a whole language curriculum. Using thumbling tales as the energizer for your unit, extend the theme through a web of related activities.

I suggest that you begin your unit by sharing several of the thumbling tales in this collection. Examine and compare them from folkloric, literary, and cultural points of view. Expand the thumbling concept with art and math projects. Screen and compare films whose plots revolve around thumbling stories. Share and compare illustrated books in which thumblings are the main character. Encourage independent reading of books featuring small heroes and create a "Who's Who" gallery of small folk from children's literature. Develop a vocabulary of words denoting diminutiveness. Explore other small creatures from folklore. Screen films dealing with diminutive creatures and discuss point of view.

Then move your study into the world of real humans of small stature. Learn about dwarfism and other causes of small stature in humans. Read about individuals of small stature. Present exercises aimed at creating empathy with smaller individuals. Take this unit further if you like into the scientific study of dwarfism in plants and animals, or into a cultural study of human groups of small stature such as the Mbuti and the San (Bushmen).

Picture Book Comparison of Thumbling Folktales

Curriculum Areas:
    Language Arts—Reading
        Folklore Literary Comparison
    Art—Art Appreciation
    Social Studies—Multicultural Study

Compare Tom Thumb Picture Books

Share several picture book treatments of the Tom Thumb story. What techniques do the artists use to denote Tom's smallness? Which illustrations do you prefer? Why?

Compare the texts of the picture books. What choices have the authors made in retelling their stories? Which are most successful?

Give a "Thumbling Award" to the Best Illustrated Tom Thumb

Consider text, illustration, and whether or not the two complement each other to produce a fine product. Use group process to decide on this award. Your class may work best in small committees, each offering its award and explaining why they selected that book.

Tom Thumb in Picture Books: A Bibliography

Brooke, Leslie. *Tom Thumb.* Illustrated by the author. London: Frederick Warne, 1904.

Grimm, Jacob and Grimm, Wilhelm. *Grimms' Tom Thumb.* Translated by Anthea Bell. Illustrated by Svend Otto. S. Larousse, 1976.

————. *Tom Thumb.* Illustrated by Felix Hoffman. New York: Atheneum, 1973.

Hillert, Margaret. *Tom Thumb.* Illustrated by Dennis Hockerman. Chicago: Follett, 1982.

Watson, Richard Jesse. *Tom Thumb.* Illustrated by the author. San Diego, CA: Harcourt, Brace, Jovanovich, 1989.

Wiesner, William. *Tom Thumb.* Illustrated by the author. New York: Walck, 1974.

Wilkinson, Barry. *The Diverting Adventures of Tom Thumb.* New York: Harcourt, Brace & World, 1969.

Other Folk Thumblings in Picture Books: A Bibliography

Bang, Betsy. *The Cucumber Stem.* Illustrated by Tony Chen. New York: Greenwillow, 1980.

Glass, Andrew. *Chickpea and the Talking Cow.* New York: Lothrop, Lee & Shepard, 1987.

Perrault, Charles. *Tom Thumb.* Adapted and illustrated by Lidia Postma. Shocken, 1983.

"Thumbelina" in Picture Books

Several illustrated picture book editions of "Thumbelina" are available in libraries and bookstores. Compare several of these. What decisions did the artists make in planning their drawings? Which do you find most successful? Notice the perspectives from which the artists look at their scenes. Are any of these especially interesting? How do the artists' styles differ? Which do you find most pleasing? Choose one scene from this story and plan an illustration for that scene. You need not draw the actual picture. Just make a quick sketch showing what elements you would include in the scene, where you would place them, and the perspective from which you would draw them.

Notice also that the texts in these editions are each slightly different. These have been translated or retold from the Danish original; as a result, no two have the same wording. Compare a few paragraphs from each text. What decisions did the translators/retellers make in choosing their words? Close the books and rewrite those paragraphs in your own style. Examine these "Thumbelina" titles.

Andersen, Hans Christian. *Thumbelina.* Illustrated by Adrienne Adams. Translated by R. P. Keigwin. New York: Charles Scribner's Sons, 1961.

Andersen, Hans Christian. *Thumbelina.* Illustrated by Wayne Anderson. Retold by James Riordan. New York: G. P. Putnam's Sons, 1991.

Andersen, Hans Christian. *Thumbelina.* Illustrated by Alison Claire Darke. New York: Doubleday, 1991.

Andersen, Hans Christian. *Thumbelina.* Illustrated by Susan Jeffers. Retold by Amy Ehrlich. New York: The Dial Press, 1979.

Issun Boshi: A Japanese Thumbling

Examine several picture book versions of the Issun Boshi story. Compare them from the point of view of cultural accuracy. In what time period in Japanese history are these tales set? What elements have the artists selected for illustration to denote that time period? Look at examples of Japanese classical painting. Do you think the artists who illustrated these Issun Boshi tales looked at paintings such as these before they began drawing?

Compare the texts of these books. The Brenners chose to invent episodes not in the traditional tale. Do you approve of this? Why or why not? Refer to the following list for Issun Boshi tales.

Issun Boshi Variants

Brenner, Barbara. *Little One Inch.* Illustrated by Fred Brenner. New York: Coward, McCann & Geoghegan, 1977.

Ishii, Momoko. *Issun Boshi: The Inchling: An Old Tale of Japan.* Translated by Yone Mizuta. Illustrated by Fuku Akino. New York: Walker and Co., 1965.

Morimoto, Junko. *The Inch Boy.* New York: Viking Kestrel, 1986.

Sakade, Florence. *Little One-Inch and Other Japanese Children's Favorite Stories.* Illustrated by Yoshisuke Kurosaki. Rutland, VT: Charles Tuttle, 1958.

Scofield, Elizabeth. *Little One Inch.* Illustrated by Ryo Arai. Paper Play series. Palo Alto, CA: Educational Progress Corporation, 1970.

Looking at Literary Uses of Thumblings

Curriculum Areas:
Language Arts—Reading
Literary Criticism
Listening Skills

Picture Books Featuring Tiny Folks

Here are some picture books featuring the adventures of tiny characters. Read several with the class. Did the authors think of unusual settings or surprising actions for their wee characters?

Beskow, Elsa Maartman. *Peter in Blueberry Land*. Edinburgh, Scotland: Floris Books, 1987.

Charming fantasy by a turn-of-the-century Swedish author.

Buffet, Savannah Jane, and Buffet, Jimmy. *Trouble Dolls*. Illustrated by Lambert Davis. San Diego, CA: Harcourt, Brace, Jovanovich, 1991.

For older readers; a picture book format but considerable text. Lizzy's Guatemalan trouble dolls (miniature dolls used as charms to take away children's troubles) help her rescue her father.

Fish, Helen Dean. *When the Root Children Wake Up*. Green Tiger Press, 1988.

A story about fairy folk who live underground. A fanciful approach reprinted from an earlier edition.

Heide, Florence Parry. *The Shrinking of Treehorn*. New York: Dell, 1961.

Reveals what happens when Treehorn begins to shrink a little each day.

Joyce, William. *George Shrinks*. Illustrated by the author. New York: Harper & Row, 1985.

George wakes up very tiny and has hair-raising adventures around the house until his parents return. A good picture book to share with preschool and primary-grade students.

Minarik, Else Holmelund. *The Little Giant Girl and the Elf Boy*.

Friendship between a giant and an elf.

Velthuijs, Max. *Little Man to the Rescue*. Translated by Rosemary Lanning. New York: Holt, 1986.

This story, along with *Little Man Finds a Home* (Holt, 1985) and *Little Man's Luck Day* (Holt, 1986), describes the adventures of a very tiny man and his animal friends.

Children's Novels Featuring Small Characters

Dahl, Roald. *The Witches*. Illustrated by Quentin Blake. New York: Farrar, Straus, Giroux, 1987.

Turned into a mouse at a witches' convention, our small hero defeats the witches after much adventure. He decides life at this size has its advantages and resigns himself contentedly to his permanent existence as a mouse. If your students are familiar with the movie version of this book you might want to discuss the difference in endings. In the movie the boy regains his human form. Ask the students which ending they prefer. What does the choice made by the filmmakers tell us about their attitude toward people who are out of the norm?

How do the filmmakers' attitudes differ from that of author Roald Dahl?

Kästner, Eric. *Little Man and the Big Thief*. Illustrated by Stanley Mack. New York: Alfred A. Knopf, 1969.

This is the translation of a German children's novel featuring a wee trickster.

Norton, Mary. *The Rescuers*. Illustrated by Garth Williams. New York: Little, Brown, 1959.

Miss Bianca and her sidekick Bernard lead the mouse Prisoner's Aid Society in many daring adventures in the huge world of humans.

O'Brien, Robert. *Mrs. Frisby and the Rats of NIMH*. New York: Atheneum, 1971.

A group of rats take on the scientists of the NIMH laboratory.

Steig, William. *Abel's Island*. Illustrated by the author. New York: Farrar, Straus, Giroux, 1976.

Mouse Abel finds himself alone on an island and unable to reach the mainland. He tries everything possible for his small size.

White, T. H. *Stuart Little*. Illustrated by Garth Williams. New York: Harper & Row, 1945.

The story of a mouse child born to a human family.

Learning about Small Characters from Folklore

Curriculum Areas:
   Language Arts—Folk Literature
       Vocabulary
   Social Studies—Multicultural Studies

Learn about other Small Characters Found in Folk Literature

Notice that our thumblings are usually not fairy creatures, but are simply very tiny humans born to ordinary parents. However some teachers may want to explore the small creatures of the fairy world. Here is a listing of wee fairy creatures. You might want to divide the class into teams and let each team research a fairy creature. Keep in mind that much material may be available on creatures such as elves, whereas it may be more difficult for your students to research lesser known creatures such as the kobald, nisse, or knocker. To learn about these creatures look them up in an unabridged dictionary and in *Funk &*

Wagnalls Standard Dictionary of Folklore, Mythology, and Legend by Maria Leach (New York: Funk and Wagnalls, 1972) or in *An Encyclopedia of Fairies, Hobgoblins, Brownies, Bogies, and Other Supernatural Creatures* by Katherine Briggs (New York: Pantheon Books, 1976).

To find stories about these creatures consult: *The Storyteller's Sourcebook: A Subject, Title, and Motif-Index to Children's Folklore Collections* by Margaret Read MacDonald (Detroit: Neal-Schuman/Gale Research, 1982).

Wee creatures from folklore to research:

Boggart	Knocker
Brownie	Leprechaun
Dwarf	Pixie
Elf	Nisse
Fairy	Nixie
Gnome	Sprite
Kobold	

Comparing Folktale Thumblings

Curriculum Areas:
    Social Studies—Multicultural Study
    Language Arts—Folklore
        Literary Comparison
        Reading

Compare Folktale Variants from Several Cultures

Read at least three Tom Thumb tales, selecting variants of different ethnic origin.

In what ways are these tales similar?

What are their most striking differences?

How does each culture mark the story with its own distinct features? "Lipunishka" (Russia), "Issun Boshi" or "The Snail Choja" (Japan), and "Little Thumb Conquers the Sun" (Burma) might be good choices for such comparison.

If you were to retell a Tom Thumb story set in your own community, could you give the tale some distinctive elements that would show that it had been told in your cultural area, or even in you own town?

Create a Folktale Comparison Chart

Make a wall chart to track the differences in the tales you read. List in columns such topics as "Thumbling's Size"; "Thumbling-Male/Female"; "Objects used by Thumbling"; "Thumbling's Special Attributes"; "Adversary"; "Actions"; and "Conclusion." Fill in the blanks for each tale you read.

Encourage students to do independent reading in thumbling tales and share the variants they discover with the class. Add them to the chart.

As you conclude your studies, examine the chart. Are certain patterns more popular than others? Did some of the tales show you unexpected variations? Are certain patterns typical of specific cultures?

Thumbling Folktales to Read

"Kernel" in *Portuguese Fairy Tales* by Maurice and Pamela Michael. Chicago: Follett, 1965, pp. 112-17.

    A Portuguese thumbling is eaten by a cow and wolf but manages to trick mule drivers and thieves.

"Little Cricket" in *Picture Tales from the French* by Simone Chamoud, New York: Frederick A. Stokes, 1983.

    A very small hero is inserted into Type 1641 *Doctor Know-All.*

"Little Finger" in *Gianni and the Ogre* by Ruth Manning-Sanders. New York: Dutton, 1970, pp. 127-40.

    This Italian thumbelina receives from four fairy godmothers gifts of beauty, voice, early speech, and the promise to come when in need. A prince hears thumbling singing and vows he will marry her.

"Little Finger of the Watermelon Patch" in *The Brocaded Slipper and Other Vietnamese Tales* by Lynette Dyer Vuong. Illustrated by Vo-Dinh Mai. New York: Lippincott, 1982, pp. 27-43.

    Parents lose their tiny girl when she falls asleep in a bamboo stalk. Youngest prince finds her and she performs suitor tasks as if she were his fiancee. Eventually she reveals that she is an enchanted fairy and turns herself into a beautiful young woman to wed Prince Hau.

"Pete and the Ox" in *Italian folktales,* by Italo Calvino. Translated by George Martin. New York: Harcourt Brace Jovanovich, 1980, pp. 334-37.

    A potful of chickpeas becomes babies. One survives to become a thumbling.

"The Tiny God" in *The Magic Listening Cap: More Folk Tales from Japan* by Yoshiko Uchida. New York: Harcourt, Brace & World, 1955, pp. 113-21.

A one-inch god from over the sea teaches a prince about silk culture, farming, and medicine.

A Thumbling Map

Curriculum Areas:
Social Studies—Map Study

Use a World Map to Locate the Countries of Origin for Your Tales

Post a map of the world on the wall. Stick pins into the countries or ethnic areas from which you have discovered thumbling tales.

Thumbling Paper Dolls

Curriculum Areas:
Social Studies—Ethnic Studies
Art

Make Thumbling Paper Dolls

Use costume books, illustrated picture books, or texts about various cultures to design costumes for your thumblings. Make thumbling paper dolls and draw on ethnic costume. Though many children around the world dress today in contemporary clothing, most cultures still depict their folk characters in the garments of an earlier era. Issun Boshi, for example, is always depicted in kimono and sword.

Comparing Thumbling Videos

Curriculum Areas:
Language Arts—Drama
Literary Criticism
Visual Literacy
Art—Film Appreciation

Screen and Compare Two Video or 16mm Versions of "Tom Thumb" or "Thumbelina"

Be sure to share the story first so that your students are familiar with the traditional Tom Thumb and the authored Thumbelina as written by Hans Christian Andersen.

The Faerie Tale Theatre renditions take liberties with their material, introducing a great deal of humor into their versions. What changes do they make to the traditional tales to create a humorous vehicle for well-known actors? Are these changes always effective? Which work best?

If you were a parent which videos would you take home for your child to watch? Why?

Some Video Versions of Thumbling Tales

Thumbelina. Rabbit Ears Storybook Classics. SVS, 1989. 30 minutes.

Thumbelina. Faerie Tale Theatre. Platypus Productions, 1983; CBS/Fox, 1987. 50 minutes.

Tom Thumb. WorldVision Home Video, 1991. 30 minutes.

Tom Thumb. Faerie Tale Theatre. Platypus Productions, 1983; CBS/Fox 1987. 50 minutes.

Learning to Tell a Thumbling Tale

Curriculum Areas:
Language Arts—Listening Skills
Memory Training
Structural Analysis of Literature
Oral Interpretation
Performance Skills

Tell a Thumbling Tale

Share a thumbling tale through storytelling. Some of these tales work well as orally told tales. Try: "Hasan, the Heroic Mouse-Child," "Loud Mouth Thummas," "Issun Boshi," and "Little Thumb Conquers the Sun."

Teach Your Students to Tell a Thumbling Tale

Follow these steps to pass a tale on to your students.

1. You tell the story.
2. Go over the story slowly again. Make sure the class notes each step in the thumbling's action. Have them repeat with you any key chants or phrases that are important to the story.
3. Break the class into groups of 3 or 4 students. Count off from 1-4 within each group. Each group will tell the entire story, passing it around their circle. Make sure they sit in a circle facing each other and tell the story *to* each other. Make sure those not telling practice good listening skills to support their teller.

   Clap your hands as a signal that student #1 should begin telling. After a bit, clap your hands again and call out "Person number 2, begin telling!" At this point the first teller stops and the second teller picks up the story right where the first teller left off. Keep this up until the story has passed around the circle. Make sure everyone gets a chance to tell.
4. After the story has been completed, let each group talk among themselves about a good way to present this story for another class. Some possible ways to present the story are:

   A. Each tell a portion of the tale, just as they have been doing in this learning session.

   B. One could tell and the others could act out the story.

   C. Some could speak the parts and others could act them out.

   If the group members opt for acting out the story rather than straight storytelling, be sure that they speak it as "story theatre." In other words each character is "telling" his or her part. For example, Tom would say: "And Tom said, 'Look what you've done!' and Tom climbed down from the roof." Each actor is *telling* about his or her action as it is being acted out.

5. Suggest that each child tell this story at home.
6. Send story teams from your class to other classes to share their stories. Give them a bit of time on the day of their storytelling performance to rehearse.

Dramatic Play

Curriculum Areas:
   Language Arts—Drama

Teams Improvise Thumbling Scenes

1. Divide into teams.
2. Each team picks two "tool" cards and two "transportation" cards. These are cards prepared by you with single words written on them. The "tool" cards name objects that a thumbling could use as tools or for defense. The "transportation" cards name objects that a thumbling could use to travel.

   Sample tool cards (you can think of more):

Rubber band	Drinking straw
Needle	Thread
Mirror	Fork
Rubber cement	Marbles
Bubble gum	Banana
Pencil	Paper napkin

   Sample transportation cards:

Orange	Umbrella
Ball	Leaf
Hat	Rope
Bowl	Roller skate
Paper cup	

   If working with children with low reading skills be sure to draw a picture of the object on the card along with the object's name.

   The teams can use these objects in any way they wish. The "tool" and "transportation" categories are only hints.
3. Each team creates a story about a small character.

The team decides who this character is.

The character meets an opponent.

The team decides who the opponent is.

The thumbling character travels, using objects they have drawn from the pack of cards.

The thumbling defeats its opponent, using objects they have drawn from the pack.

4. After the team has created their story, the team practices acting it out. They may create dialogue to speak as they act out the story, or they may assign one team member to narrate the adventure while the others act it out.

5. The team performs for the class. Before beginning their drama, each team should explain who their characters are, who is playing which roles, and what objects they will be using. They should not explain *how* they plan to use the objects at this point though.

Writing a Thumbling Story

Curriculum Areas:
Language Arts—Creative Writing

Guided Outlining of a Thumbling Story

This activity should be attempted after the students have heard a variety of thumbling stories. Provide students with two brightly colored pieces of paper. On one piece of paper students write the names of the characters about whom they plan to write. On the second piece of paper students list in order of occurrence the events in their story, using single words. This paper should be cut long and narrow to encourage *listing*.

Display a sample list for the students:
Sample Characters Could Be:

Issun Boshi
Ogre
Princess

Sample Events Might Include

Hero born
Travels

Meets princess
Travels
Meets ogre
Defeats ogre with needle
Marries princess

After outlining the story in this way, the students are ready to begin writing.

Creative Writing from a Thumbling's Perspective

Curriculum Areas:
Language Arts—Creative Writing

Imagining Smallness: A Creative Writing Plan

Give the students these instructions:

Imagine you are very small.

Choose a size.

Get a ruler and measure off a "person" just that size.

Cut a piece of paper to that length and draw your tiny self on that paper.

Place this "self" next to various objects in the room, a desk, a sink, a book, etc. Imagine how it would feel to be that size. How would the objects around you look from your small person point of view?

Write a few paragraphs from your "small person" perspective. Describe what you see . . . feel . . . smell . . . hear from your small-size outlook on life.

Write some more paragraphs about your small person. Give the person a problem . . . making a phone call . . . fixing breakfast . . . . Tell how that person solves the problem.

Place your small person in a dangerous situation, then get the thumbling out of it. Did your thumbling use force, trickery, clever inventions, arbitration?

Reward your small person. What would he or she want as a reward? To be bigger? To stay the same size? To find friends who are the same size? Riches? A tiny palace?

Learning Thumbling Terms

Curriculum Areas:
  Language Arts—Dictionary Skills
    Vocabulary

Give Each Child a Word to Explore

Let the student present their word and its meaning to the class.

Bonsai	Minikin
Diminish	Minimum
Diminutive	Minimize
Dwarf (verb)	Minute
Dwindle	Minutiae
Infinitesimal	Mite
Imp	Molecular
Impish	Nanism
Lilliputian	Paltry
Manikin	Puny
Microscopic	Pygmy (noun)
Midge	Pygmy (adjective)
Midget	Runt
Miniature	Wee

Thumbling Terms from Other Languages

Curriculum Areas:
  Language Arts—Dictionary Skills
    Vocabulary
    Other Languages
  Social Studies—Multicultural Study

Learn Thumbling Terms used in Other Languages

Look up these thumbling terms from other languages. Here are many ways to say "small."

Chiisai (Japanese)
Klein (German)
Let (Thai)
Liten (Norwegian)
Nid (Thai)
Nio (Thai)
Pequeño (Spanish)
Petit (French)
Piccolo (Italian)
Smälig (Norwegian)

Films from a Thumbling Perspective

Curriculum Areas:
  Language Arts—Visual Literacy
    Scripting
  Art—Film Study

View and Discuss Films Treating a Thumbling Perspective

Film should be studied with the same serious intent that is devoted to other literary and artistic genres. Share these remarkable films with your students.

After screening several films consider these points:

How did the filmmaker present the small creature's perspective?

Which films were most successful in making the viewer empathize with the tiny creature? Why do you think these were so successful?

What filmic techniques were used in the films screened? "Captain Silas" and "Hank the Cave Peanut" use object animation, "Tin Toy" uses computer animation, "Why'd the Beetle Cross the Road?" is live action, the others are animated through drawing.

Which do you prefer? What are the strong points of each technique?

Some Films from a Small Perspective

Captain Silas. Barr Films, 1977. 14 min.
    Peanut animation.
Cosmic Zoom. McGraw-Hill, 1970. 8 min.
    From outer space to inner space and back.
Hank the Cave Peanut. Yellow Bison, 1975. 15 min.
    Another film in which household objects are used innovatively by peanut people.

Some Films through the Eyes of Small Creatures

Dr. DeSoto. Weston Woods, 1984. 9 min.
    To a mouse dentist a fox patient is . . .
Self Service. COF, 1975. 10 min.
    To a mosquito a big toe is . . . ? (For older audiences)
Smile for Auntie. Weston Woods, 1979. 4 min.
    To a baby a fond auntie is . . . ?
Snookles. Pyramid, 1987. 2 min.
    To a dragon a baby bird is . . . ? (Preview before showing. Not for the very young.)
Tin Toy. Direct Cinema, 1988. 4 min.
    To a wind-up toy a baby is . . . ?
Why'd the Beetle Cross the Road? Pyramid, 1985. 8 min.
    To a beetle the California beach scene is . . . ?

Stories on Film about Small Creatures

Ben and Me. Walt Disney, 1953. 21 min.
    The mouse behind Ben Franklin's success.
Stuart Little. McGraw-Hill, 1969. 58 min.
    A mouse child copes with a huge world.
Teeny-Tiny and the Witch Woman. Weston Woods, 1980. 14 min.
    Folktale of the youngest brother who saves his elder siblings.

A Mystery Film

Zea. National Film Board of Canada, 1981. 5 min.
    A close-up of a very small object. Let the audience guess what it might be as the film progresses. (You must preview this yourself to find out what it is!) Even preschool children enjoy trying to guess this one.

Creating Thumbling Pictures

Curriculum Areas:
    Art

Create a Thumbling Picture

Provide the children with a pile of old magazines or pictures precut from magazines. Give each a photocopied thumbling to be cut out as a tiny paper doll.

The children select an object from the pictures that could be used by their thumbling. Then they paste the object chosen onto a piece of paper and paste on the thumbling, showing the thumbling in action using the object.

Example: Paste on a picture of a toaster. Then paste on a thumbling sliding down the toaster side.

If you have time, let each student create a booklet of such pictures showing their thumblings at play among various household objects.

A Thumbling Diorama

Curriculum Areas:
    Art

Make a Thumbling Diorama

You may use a shoebox, but a piece of cardboard folded in half works fine, one half is the floor, the other the back wall. For younger children this open space is easier to work with than an enclosed shoebox. Older children enjoy the enclosed world of the shoebox.

Provide an assortment of objects that could be used imaginatively in creating a small environment for a thumbling. Yarn, thread, cotton balls, Easter basket grass, marbles, walnut shells, small boxes, stick-on dots, craft feathers, tiny pom poms are excellent materials to have on hand.

Make a thumbling from three pieces of pipe cleaner. Hold two pipe cleaners together and wrap the third around these to form arms. Fold out the bottom half of the two body pipe cleaners to form legs. Apply two stick-on dots back to back onto the top of the two body pipe cleaners to form a head and draw on a face.

Studying Size and Measurement

Curriculum Areas:
    Math

Thinking about Size

Pass out a worksheet on which you have drawn onto large square graph paper three tables and chairs of varying sizes. Pass out three paper doll patterns of varying sizes designed to fit the furniture. Ask the children to paste the dolls next to the furniture that fits the doll's size.

Thinking about Measurement

Using a doll, decide how tall a table should be to serve that doll. How tall should the doll's chair be? Measure from the floor to the doll's waist and from the floor to her outstretched hand. Write down suggested heights for countertops, tables, chairs, etc., for this doll's house.

Design a room to scale: Assume that the average piece of furniture is designed to fit a person 6 feet tall. Design a room with furniture for a person 3 feet tall. Indicate the height of tables, chairs, beds, etc. **OR** Design a room for a person 6 inches tall. Use graph paper to draw this room. **OR** Make a model of a room for a person 6 inches tall.

A Small Stature Relay Race

Curriculum Areas:
    Physical Activity
    Social Studies—Social Awareness

Plan a Table Setting Relay: Too Short to Reach!

Consider how it would feel to be too short to reach a tabletop comfortably.

You will need: two tables for each team; two place settings including knives, forks, spoons, napkins, plastic plates, and plastic glasses; one pitcher full of water; one bowlful of frozen peas; and a serving spoon.

Walking on knees the first student takes the silverware and napkin from the first table, carries them to the second table, and sets two places. The student then returns and fills two glasses with water and takes them to the second table. The student returns and fills a plate with frozen peas and takes it to the second table.

The second student, walking on knees also, takes the glasses back and empties the water back into the pitcher, retrieves the plate and returns the peas to the bowl, and brings the place settings back to the first table.

Repeat with as many students as you have on your team. Set up as many tables as you need for the teams you wish to compete.

The tables need not be far apart. This is not a knee-walking exercise but an upper body stretching exercise.

Learning about Dwarfism

Curriculum Areas:
    Science

Learn about Dwarfism in Humans, Plants, and Animals

Within the range of human size, some individuals are much smaller than others. Read books on the scientific causes of dwarfism in humans, animals, and plants.

Discussing the Use of Growth Hormones

Curriculum Areas:
    Science
    Social Studies—Social Issues

With Your Class, Explore the use of Growth Hormones

Children with the growth deficiency known as pituitary dwarfism are sometimes given growth hormones that cause them to attain greater height. But there is medical debate over these hormones. Read articles on the controversy and discuss this matter. Consult the subject heading "Dwarfism, Pituitary" in your periodical indexes for more recent articles.

Suggested Articles

"Ethical Issues in Growth Hormone Therapy" by John Dantos, Mark Siegler, and Leona Cuttler. *The Journal of the American Medical Association.* (February 17, 1989): p. 1070. (5 pages). Very technical.

"Gennentech's Drug Problems: The Perils of Marketing a Synthetic Hormone. (Protropin)" by Pamela

Abramson. *Newsweek.* 106 (November 25, 1985): p. 70.

"The Growing Danger from Gene-spliced Hormones" by Thomas Murray. *Discover* (February 1987): p. 88. (3 pages)

"Short-stature Treatment Reevaluated" by Joanne Silberner. *Science News.* 128 (August 17, 1985): p. 103.

Discussing Size and Social Relationships

Curriculum Areas:
    Social Studies—Social Relationships

With Your Students Discuss the Way Size Influences our Social Relationships

All size is relative. You are much smaller than some people. You are much larger than others. Make a word list of feelings you have in the presence of people much larger than yourself. Make a word list of feelings you have in the presence of people much smaller than yourself. Examine the words in your list and compare them with those of others in the class. Are the words based on physical reality? Are any of them based on an unrealistic fear or prejudice? Have there been times when your expectation for encounters with a larger or with a smaller individual proved wrong?

Thinking about People Who Are Small

Curriculum Areas:
    Science
    Social Studies—Social Relationships

Meet Jaime Osborn, the Smallest Kid in Her Class

Read the excellent photo-essay account of eight-year-old Jaime Osborn in *Thinking Big: The Story of a Young Dwarf* by Susan Kuklin (New York: Lothrop, Lee & Shepard, 1986). The book gives clear information about the genetic causes of aconoplastic dwarfism and discusses possible medical problems encountered by little people. Jaime's successful attempts to cope with her difference are documented. This is an upbeat portrait of a charming young girl.

This book defines "dwarf" as an individual with an average size body and smaller than usual limbs. "Midget" is defined as an individual who is of usual proportions but is very small.

Ask your students to put themselves in Jaime's place: What social problems do you think Jaime might encounter? If Jaime was in your class, what could you do to make her feel at home.

How can a very small person succeed in an overwhelmingly large world?

What techniques did your thumblings use to succeed? Trickery? Perseverance?

What other techniques might a small person use? Arbitration? Kindness? Wisdom?

Do the solutions of the folktales work in the real world? Why do you think we like to hear these thumbling tales?

What techniques have small persons used in the past to make their way in the world? Being friendly? Keeping a low profile? Becoming a martinet? Playing the clown?

Learning more about people who are very small: Very small individuals tend to get relegated to certain roles in society. There is a tendency to consider dwarf and midget individuals as cute, doll-like, and comical. The little people whom the public see most often and are most familiar with are those who enter the entertainment field. Some well-known small actors are Herve Villechaize who played Tatoo in the television program "Fantasy Island," the many dwarfs employed in the making of "The Wizard of Oz," and TV's Gary Coleman, star of "Different Strokes," whose short stature is due to a kidney implant at an early age. Little people who make careers in other occupations such as teaching or business have to constantly cope with the notion of the public that they should be "cute" and "entertaining."

To learn more about little people the teacher might examine these books:

The Challenges Facing Dwarf Parents: Preparing for a New Baby by Ellen Highland Fernandez. Tamarac, FL: Distinctive Publishing, 1989. (P.O. Box 26941, Tamarac, FL 33321)

This small handbook for dwarf parents on the care of children was written by a young woman who is herself an aconoplastic dwarf. The book looks at the problems she encountered in raising her daughter. A useful book to develop empathy with dwarf parents. Fernandez talks about her encounters with well-meaning children who insist that she is too small to be allowed to handle a baby.

Living with Difference: Families with Dwarf Children by Joan Ablon. New York: Praeger, 1988.

An in-depth text on the problems and pleasures of surviving as a little person, with special emphasis on helping families cope with the addition of a smaller than usual child to their family. Addresses for Little People of America organizations around the country are given. The book includes a detailed and technical bibliography.

Becoming Sensitive to the Terms We Use

Curriculum Areas:
    Language Arts—Vocabulary
    Social Studies—Social Relationships

Examine the Terms We Use to Talk about Smallness

Look for more sensitive ways to speak. The Random House Dictionary says of a "dwarf": "A dwarf is one checked in growth or stunted; he usually has a large head or is in some way not normally formed. In the past dwarfs were considered very comical."

Sometimes we are insensitive to other people's feelings just in the language we use to talk about them. Compare the way two different dictionaries define "dwarf." Do they seem sensitive or insensitive in their definitions? How do you think

Jaime would feel when she read the definition above? Write a more sensitive definition based on what you have learned about dwarfism.

Discuss the saying "I felt very small." Have you heard people use this expression? What did they mean by that? Look up "small . . . feel small" in Roget's *Thesaurus*. What synonyms are given for "feel small"?

Reading Biographies of Small Individuals

Curriculum Areas:
    Social Science—Biography
    Language Arts—Reading

Read and Share Biographies about Persons of Small Stature

The Real Tom Thumb by Helen Reeder Cross. New York: Four Winds Press, 1980.

An appealing biography of Charles Sherwood Stratton, the famous General Tom Thumb of P. T. Barnum's American Museum in nineteenth-century New York. Born in 1838, Stratton was taken to New York by Barnum at the age of four and was one of Barnum's main attractions until his death in 1883. Readable text (grades 3-6), enhanced with photographs and illustrated by Stephen Gammell.

Have You Seen Tom Thumb? by Mabel Leigh Hunt. Philadelphia, PA: J. B. Lippincott, 1942.

A partially fictionalized biography of Charles Stratton and his wife, Lavinia Warren.

Gary Coleman: Medical Miracle by Bill Davidson and the Coleman family. New York: Coward McCann & Geoghegan, 1981.

This is an adult book, but portions could be shared with your students. Each chapter is followed by first-person quotes from Gary, his mom, and his dad, showing their own reactions to their experiences.

Sample Public Library Thumbling Programs

Preschool

- Talk about how it would feel to be very small.
- Read *Little Man to the Rescue* by Max Velthuijs (New York: North-South Books, 1986). Frog finds a note in a bottle and climbs in to retrieve it. "Help! Help!" it says. Little Man and Frog go to the rescue.
- Talk about being small enough to climb into a bottle. Read the book *In the Night Kitchen* by Maurice Sendak (New York: Harper & Row, 1970) about a boy who swims in a milk bottle.
- Read *A Worm's Tale* by Barbro Lindgren; illustrated by Cecilia Torudd (Stockholm: R & S Books, 1988). In this book Arthur, a staid, lonely gentleman, takes up with a friendly worm. Have the children sit in a circle, then put a basket full of small objects in the center of the circle. Each child can choose one object to hold. The child decides how a tiny person (or a worm) would use that object. (Suggested objects: nutshell, matchbox, spool, string, candy cane, saucer, shell, facial tissue, etc.)
- Sing: (To the tune of "I'm not small")

  I'm so small.
  I'm so small.
  I can use a matchbox for a bed.

  Invent many verses using the pattern "I can use a _____ for a _____."
- Read a story about a little girl *pretending* to be as small as a bug. In *A House of Leaves* by Kiyoshi Soya; illustrated by Akiko Hayashi (New York: Philomel Books, 1986) a little girl hides from the rain in a leafy cave in the bushes. Insects join her in her "house."
- Make a campsite for a worm. Fold a piece of paper (3" x 1") in half to form a tent. Fold each side of the tent up ¼" at the bottom and apply glue to stick it onto a piece of poster board. Break two toothpicks in half and paste them onto the board to form campfire logs. Glue on a dab of green Easter basket grass for bushes. Curl a 3" piece of pipe cleaner into a worm. Add two stick-on dots pasted back to back on the pipe cleaner's end as a head. Draw on eyes.

Grades K-3

- Provide a display of thumbling books.
- Talk about how it would feel to be very small. Let the children suggest ideas about how a thumbling would travel and how he or she would set up a home.
- Talk about thumbling stories and ask the group to suggest thumbling stories they have heard or read.
- Tell a thumbling story. Especially tellable stories in this collection are "Loud Mouth Thummas," "Little Thumb Conquers the Sun," and "Issun Boshi."
- Read a thumbling picture book. See list on page 155.
- Create a thumbling play. See DRAMATIC PLAY page 160.
- Make a thumbling diorama. This is a fun activity that can occupy children for quite a long time. For instructions see page 163.
- Program length: 1 hour (though allowing an extra 15 minutes for enthusiastic diorama builders would be a good idea!)

Grades 4–6

- Prepare a display of books featuring miniature characters.
- Discuss thumbling characters familiar to the group.
- Book talk several novels, such as *The Borrowers* by Mary Norton, *The Rescuers* by Margery Sharp, and the *The Gammage Cup* by Carol Kendal. See page 157 for these and other juvenile novels.

- Tell a Tom Thumb story. From this collection try "Loud Mouth Thummas," "Hasan, the Heroic Mouse-Child," or "Issun Boshi." "The Snail Choja," with its romantic theme, may have more appeal for older (Grade 6+) listeners.
- Perform a dramatic play. See page 160 for creative drama suggestions.
- Write a short thumbling tale. See page 161 for suggested activities.

More Miniature Life-style Books to Share

Goffstein, Brooke. *Our Prairie Home: A Picture Album*. New York: Harper & Row, 1988.
  An antique dollhouse tale.

Hurd, Thatcher. *The Pea Patch Jig*. New York: Crown, 1986.
  Mice in a huge vegetable patch.
Lionni, Leo. *Inch by Inch*. New York: Astor, 1960.
  A tiny worm in a big world.
Oakley, Graham. *The Church Mouse*. New York: Atheneum, 1972.
  Mice in a British cathedral.
Peppe, Rodney. *The Mice and the Flying Basket*. New York: Lothrop, Lee & Shepard, 1985.
  Mice use a basket as a flying machine.
Potter, Beatrix. *The Tale of Two Bad Mice*. London: Frederick Warne, 1904.
  Two mice wreck a doll house.

Multicultural Index

Bibliography of Works Consulted

This bibliography includes a few scholarly works not mentioned in this book. Several thumbling tales discussed are in obscure texts that the classroom teacher would not be able to access with ease, so they are not included in the Tale Notes. However, they do appear here and the page number on which a thumbling tale appears is noted for use by future thumbling scholars.

Aarne, Antti. *The Types of the Folktales: A Classification and Bibliography.* Translated and enlarged by Stith Thompson. Helsinki: Suomalainen Tiedeakatemia, Academia Scientiarum Fennica, 1973.

Ablon, Joan. *Living with Difference: Families with Dwarf Children.* New York: Praeger, 1988.

Arnott, Kathleen. *African Myths & Legends.* New York: Henry Z. Walck, 1962.

Ashabranner, Brent and Davis, Russell. *The Lion's Whiskers.* Boston: Little, Brown and Co., 1959.

Bang, Betsy. *The Cucumber Stem.* Illustrated by Tony Chen. New York: Greenwillow, 1980.

Briggs, Katherine. *Encyclopedia of British Folk-Literature.* Bloomington: Indiana University Press, 1970.
> Contains "The History of Tom Thumb," pp. 531–33.

———. *An Encyclopedia of Fairies, Hobgoblins, Brownies, Bogies, and Other Supernatural Creatures.* New York: Pantheon, 1976.

Calvino, Italo. *Italian Folktales.* Translated by George Martin. New York: Harcourt, Brace, Jovanovich, 1980.
> Contains "Pete and the Ox," pp. 334–37.

Carey, Bonnie. *Baba Yaga's Geese and Other Russian Stories.* Bloomington: Indiana University Press, 1973.

Chamoud, Simone. *Picture Tales from the French.* New York: Frederick Stokes, 1933.
> Contains "Little Cricket."

Chase, Richard. *Grandfather Tales.* Boston: Houghton Mifflin, 1948.

———. *Jack Tales.* Boston: Houghton Mifflin, 1946.

Christiansen, Reidar. *Folktales of Norway.* Translated by Pat Shaw Iversen. Chicago: University of Chicago Press, 1964.

Cross, Helen Reeder. *The Real Tom Thumb.* New York: Four Winds Press, 1980.

Dasent, George Webb. *East o' the Sun and West o' the Moon. Fifty-nine Norwegian Folktales from the Collection of Peter Christen Asbjörnsen and Jörgen Moe.* Edinburgh, Scotland: David Douglas, 1888.

Davidson, Bill and the Coleman family. *Gary Coleman: Medical Miracle.* New York: Coward McCann & Geoghegan, 1981.

Eastman, Mary Huse. *Index to Fairy Tales, Myths and Legends.* Boston: F. W. Faxon, 1926.

———. *Supplement.* Boston: F. W. Faxon, 1937.

———. *2nd Supplement.* Boston: F. W. Faxon, 1952.

Eugenio, Damiana L. *Philippine Folk Literature: The Folktales.* Quezon City, Philippines: U. P. Folklorists, Inc., in cooperation with the Philippine National Science Society, 1989.
> Contains "Carancal," pp. 192–93; "Baut," pp. 199–200.

Fernandez, Ellen Highland. *The Challenges Facing Dwarf Parents: Preparing for a New Baby.* Tamarac, FL: Distinctive Publishing, 1989.

Fielding, Henry. *The Tragedy of Tragedies or The Life and Death of Tom Thumb the Great. With the Annotations of H. Scriblerus Secundus.* Edited by James T. Hillhouse. New Haven, CT: Yale University Press, 1918.

Fillmore, Parker. *The Laughing Prince.* New York: Harcourt, Brace & World, 1961.

Grimm, Jacob and Grimm, Wilhelm. *Grimms' Household Tales.* Translated by Margaret Hunt. In two volumes. London: George Bell and Sons, 1884.

Halliwell-Phillips, James Orchard. *Popular Rhymes and Nursery Tales.* London: John Russell Smith, 1849.
> Contains "Teeny-Tiny," pp. 25–26; "Tom Thumb," pp. 94–100.

Hansen, Terence L. *The Types of the Folktale in Cuba, Puerto Rico, the Dominican Republic, and Spanish South America.* Berkeley: University of California Press, 1957.
> Several thumbling tales are cited.

Haviland, Virginia. *Favorite Fairy Tales Told in France.* Boston: Little, Brown, 1919.

Hoogosian-Villa, Susie. *100 Armenian Tales and Their Folkloristic Relevance*. Detroit, MI: Wayne State University, 1966.

Htin Aung, Maung. *Burmese Folk Tales*. London: Oxford University Press, 1948.

Hunt, Mabel Leigh. *Have You Seen Tom Thumb?* Philadelphia, PA: J. B. Lippincott, 1942.

Hutchinson, Veronica. *Chimney Corner Fairy Tales*. New York: Minton Balch, 1926.

Ireland, Norma Olin. *Index to Fairy Tales, 1949–1972*. Westwood, MA: F. W. Faxon, 1973.

———. *Index to Fairy Tales, 1973–1977*. Westwood, MA: F. W. Faxon, 1979.

———. *Index to Fairy Tales, 1978–1986*. Westwood, MA: F. W. Faxon, 1989.

Ishii, Momoko. *Issun Boshi, the Inchling*. New York: Walker, 1965.

Jacobs, Joseph. *English Folk and Fairy Tales*. New York: Putnam, n.d.

Jagendorf, Moritz and Boggs, Ralph Steel. *King of the Mountains*. New York: Vanguard, 1960.

Kavcic, Vladimir. *The Golden Bird: Folk Tales from Slovenia*. Translated by Jan Dekker and Helen Lencek. Cleveland, OH: World, 1962.

Kuklin, Susan. *Thinking Big: The Story of a Young Dwarf*. New York: Lothrop, Lee & Shepard, 1986.

Lang, Andrew. *The Blue Fairy Book*. New York: Dover, 1965.

———. *The Yellow Fairy Book*. New York: Dover, 1966.

Leach, Maria. *The Standard Dictionary of Folklore, Mythology, and Legend*. New York: Funk & Wagnalls, 1972.

Lima, Carolyn W. and Lima, John A. *A to Zoo: Subject Access to Children's Picture Books*. 3rd ed. New York: Bowker, 1989.

MacDonald, Margaret Read. *The Storyteller's Sourcebook: A Subject, Title, and Motif Index to Folklore Collections for Children*. Detroit, MI: Neal-Schuman/Gale Research, 1982.

Macmillan, Cyrus. *Canadian Wonder Tales*. London: The Bodley Head, 1974.
Contains "The Mouse and the Sun," pp. 30–33.

Manning-Sanders. *Gianni and the Ogre*. New York: E. P. Dutton, 1970.
Contains "Little Finger," pp. 127–40.

Massignon, Geneviéve. *Folktales of France*. Chicago: University of Chicago Press, 1968.

Michael, Maurice and Michael, Pamela. *Portuguese Fairy Tales*. Chicago: Follett, 1965.
Contains "Kernel," pp. 112–17.

Morel, Alicia. *Cuentos Aruacanos: La Gente de la Tierra*. Santiago: Editorial Andres Bello, 1982.

Opie, Iona and Opie, Peter. *The Classic Fairy Tales*. London: Oxford University Press, 1974.
Contains "The History of Tom Thumb," pp. 30–46; "Hop O' My Thumb," pp. 128–36.

Perrault, Charles. *Perrault's Fairy Tales*. Translated by A. E. Johnson. New York: Dover, 1969.

Pomerantseva, E. *Northern Lights: Fairy Tales of the Peoples of the North*. English translation by Irina Zheleznova. Moscow: Progress Publishers, 1976.
Contains "The Blueberry," pp. 91–93; "Niraidak," pp. 165–68.

Saucier, Corinne L. *Folk Tales from French Louisiana*. Claitor's Publishing Division, 1962.
Contains "Poucette," pp. 49–50.

Saunieres, S. de. *Revista Chilena de Historia y Geografia*. Vol. 26, 1918.

Sawyer, Ruth. *Picture Tales from Spain*. New York: Lippincott, 1936.

Sechrist, Elizabeth Hough. *Once in the First Times: Folk Tales from the Philippines*. Philadelphia, PA: Macrae Smith, 1969.
Contains "Little Shell," pp. 93–97.

Seki, Keigo. *Folktales of Japan*. Translated by Robert J. Adams. Chicago: University of Chicago Press, 1963.
Contains "Little One Inch," pp. 90–92; "The Snail Choja," pp. 82–90.

Siddiqui, Ashraf and Lerch, Marilyn. *Toontoony Pie and Other Tales from Pakistan*. Cleveland, OH; New York: The World Publishing Company, 1961.
Contains "The Man Who Was Only Three Inches Tall," pp. 91–97.

Thompson, Stith. *Motif-Index of Folk-Literature*. 6 vols. Bloomington: Indiana University Press, 1966.

Uchida, Yoshiko. *The Dancing Kettle and Other Japanese Folktales*. New York: Harcourt, Brace, 1949.

———. *The Magic Listening Cap: More Folk Tales from Japan*. New York: Harcourt, Brace, & World, 1955.
Contains "The Tiny God," pp. 113–21.

Vuong, Lynette Dyer. *The Brocaded Slipper and Other Vietnamese Tales*. New York: Lippincott, 1982.
Contains "Little Finger of the Watermelon Patch," pp. 27–43.

Wade, Mary Hazelton. *Indian Fairy Tales*. Great Neck, NY: Core Collection, 1979.

Walker, Barbara K. *A Treasury of Turkish Folktales for Children*. Hamden, CT: Linnet, 1988.

Index

by Janet Perlman